About This Book

Why is this topic important?

Mobile devices are here, there, and everywhere. Can we use them to support learning? The answer is a definite "yes"! Mobile provides a new channel for learning—whether it be formal or informal—and offers unique properties for just-in-time, just-in-place learning. Mobile is not just about courses, but instead supports a broad definition of learning, including innovation, collaboration, research, design, and more, generating new products, services, and problems solved. Whether providing needed tools, augmenting learning, or connecting individuals, mobile is a powerful new tool for supporting performance.

What can you achieve with this book?

This book provides a comprehensive basis for you to take advantage of mobile learning. It approaches mobile learning from a fundamental perspective, helping you understand and appreciate the rich opportunities that mLearning presents. The book briefly reviews the history of learning from a broad perspective and then goes on to survey the breadth of devices available in today's market, equipping you with appropriate ways to think about and pursue mobile learning. mLearning requires some new perspectives, and a variety of ways to think differently about the opportunities are presented to help shake up your thinking in productive ways. The book addresses the process of designing, delivering, and deploying mobile solutions, along with organizational pragmatics, to guide you through your mobile projects. Finally, discussions of strategic implications and a review of coming directions keep you prepared for the future. Examples help ground the concepts throughout the book.

How is the book organized?

This book is designed as the key resource for those interested in mobile learning, or mLearning. It is primarily intended for those involved in organizational learning, but is also designed to serve as both a guide for institutional learning and as a textbook.

The coverage is intended to address mLearning at both a conceptual and pragmatic level. At the conceptual level, the book provides frameworks about learning and performance support at the top level and in a wide variety of less comprehensive ways to think about mobile learning. At the pragmatic level, the book provides both examples and tools to help guide mobile design.

The book is organized into four sections: a brief introduction about why mLearning is important, a deep dive into the foundational knowledge you need to be ready to "think" mLearning, detail around the pragmatics of mobile development, and finally some of the larger context and trends and developments to be aware of. Within each of these sections are chapters that reflect major categories of information to be covered. The four sections and fourteen chapters are outlined below:

I. *Why mLearning* introduces the topic via:

   1. *Overview* of why mLearning

   2. *Details* elaborates on that overview

II. *Foundations* provides a broad coverage of ways to think about mLearning:

   3. *A Brief History of Learning and Cognition* revisits learning

   4. *The Technology It's Not About* provides an overview of mobile devices

   5. *Getting Contextual* looks at mobile learning in various settings

   6. *Getting Concrete* provides a number of elaborated examples

   7. *Mobile Models* presents a wide variety of ways to conceptualize mLearning

III. *Brass Tacks* gets into pragmatics of mLearning

   8. *A Platform to Stand On* presents the benefits of an infrastructure approach

   9. *Mobile Design* provides coverage of analysis and design

   10. *The Development It's Not About* covers development issues

   11. *Implementation and Evaluation* discusses implementation and organizational issues

IV. *Looking Forward* provides a strategic view and coming trends

    12. *Being Strategic* presents a performance ecosystem view of technology in organizational learning

    13. *Trends and Directions* covers current trends and likely convergences

    14. *Get Going (Mobile)* is a call to action

The book is designed both for reading and as a reference. The first four chapters, at least, should be read to ground thinking about mobile. Readers should then decide whether they would like an overview (Chapter 5), examples (Chapter 6), or a variety of concepts (Chapter 7). Chapter 7, in particular, should be thought of as a repository of sparks to mobile thinking. The third section, Chapters 8 through 11, is to be used as a guide when an mLearning initiative is being considered.

The final section is for those who want to look at mLearning as a component of both organizational strategy and in society as a whole.

The audience for this book is not only instructional designers but also developers, media experts, managers, and anyone with responsibility for supporting performance in organizations. While the focus is largely on the design of solutions, there is enough support for the reasons to think mobile and the organizational issues to assist the larger agenda of mobilizing the organization.

There are questions at the end of most chapters that are intended for readers to check their understanding and prepare to develop and deliver mobile learning.

In addition, there is an associated website that will have resources, links, and more. For access, please access the following URL:

www.designingmlearning.com

About Pfeiffer

Pfeiffer serves the professional development and hands-on resource needs of training and human resource practitioners and gives them products to do their jobs better. We deliver proven ideas and solutions from experts in HR development and HR management, and we offer effective and customizable tools to improve workplace performance. From novice to seasoned professional, Pfeiffer is the source you can trust to make yourself and your organization more successful.

Essential Knowledge Pfeiffer produces insightful, practical, and comprehensive materials on topics that matter the most to training and HR professionals. Our Essential Knowledge resources translate the expertise of seasoned professionals into practical, how-to guidance on critical workplace issues and problems. These resources are supported by case studies, worksheets, and job aids and are frequently supplemented with CD-ROMs, websites, and other means of making the content easier to read, understand, and use.

Essential Tools Pfeiffer's Essential Tools resources save time and expense by offering proven, ready-to-use materials—including exercises, activities, games, instruments, and assessments—for use during a training or team-learning event. These resources are frequently offered in looseleaf or CD-ROM format to facilitate copying and customization of the material.

Pfeiffer also recognizes the remarkable power of new technologies in expanding the reach and effectiveness of training. While e-hype has often created whizbang solutions in search of a problem, we are dedicated to bringing convenience and enhancements to proven training solutions. All our e-tools comply with rigorous functionality standards. The most appropriate technology wrapped around essential content yields the perfect solution for today's on-the-go trainers and human resource professionals.

Pfeiffer
www.pfeiffer.com *Essential resources for training and HR professionals*

Pfeiffer

DESIGNING mLEARNING

Tapping into the Mobile Revolution for Organizational Performance

CLARK N. QUINN

Pfeiffer
A Wiley Imprint
www.pfeiffer.com

Published by Pfeiffer
An Imprint of Wiley
989 Market Street, San Francisco, CA 94103-1741
www.pfeiffer.com

For additional copies/bulk purchases of this book in the U.S. please contact 800-274-4434.

Pfeiffer books and products are available through most bookstores. To contact Pfeiffer directly call our Customer Care Department within the U.S. at 800-274-4434, outside the U.S. at 317-572-3985, fax 317-572-4002, or visit www.pfeiffer.com.

Library of Congress Cataloging-in-Publication Data
Quinn, Clark N.
   Designing mLearning : tapping into the mobile revolution for organizational performance / Clark N. Quinn.
      p. cm.
   Includes bibliographical references and index.
   ISBN 978-0-470-60448-9 (hardback); ISBN 978-0-470-94592-6 (ebk);
   ISBN 978-0-470-94593-3 (ebk); ISBN 978-0-470-94594-0 (ebk)
   1. Management—Communication systems. 2. Mobile communication systems.
   3. Organizational learning. 4. Organizational effectiveness. 5. Information technology—
   Management. 6. Employees—Training of—Computer-assisted instruction. I. Title.
     HD30.335.Q56 2011
     658.3'12404—dc22   2010043315

Pfeiffer also publishes its books in a variety of electronic formats. Some content that appears in print may not be available in electronic books.

Acquiring Editor: Matthew Davis   Production Editor: Michael Kay
Marketing Manager: Brian Grimm   Editor: Rebecca Taff
Editorial Assistant: Lindsay Morton   Manufacturing Supervisor: Becky Morgan

Printed in the United States of America

Printing   10 9 8 7 6 5 4 3 2 1

CONTENTS

Figures and Tables   xv

Foreword   xix

Preface   xxiii

Acknowledgements   xxv

SECTION I: WHY MLEARNING

CHAPTER ONE: OVERVIEW   3

CHAPTER TWO: THE DETAILS   7

    Misconceptions   8

    The Business Case   10

    Questions to Ask   12

SECTION II: FOUNDATIONS

CHAPTER THREE: A BRIEF HISTORY OF LEARNING
AND COGNITION   15

    Formal Learning   19

    Media Psychology   23

    Beyond Cognition   24

    Informal Learning   25

    Social Learning   27

    Questions to Ask   28

CHAPTER FOUR: THE TECHNOLOGY IT'S NOT
ABOUT   29

    From the Calculator to the Smartphone   30

    The Convergent Model   41

    Come Together   49

    Questions to Ask   50

CHAPTER FIVE: GETTING CONTEXTUAL   51

    K12   52

    Higher Ed   55

    Organizational   56

    Nonformal   57

    The Global Perspective   58

    Questions to Ask   59

An Interview with Mobile Learning Leader Judy Brown   61

CHAPTER SIX: GETTING CONCRETE   63

    Learning Augment   64

    Pharmaceutical Sales   65

    Flexible Delivery   70

    Multiplatform Mobile Simulation/Game Templates   74

    Addressing STEM via Mobile   76

    Making Mobile at St. Marys   81

    Learning WWW (Wherever Whenever and Whatever)   85

    Ubiquitous Games   88

    Summary   93

An Interview with Mobile Learning Leader David Metcalf   95

CHAPTER SEVEN: MOBILE MODELS   97

    The Four C's of Mobile Capability   98

    Being Opportunistic   104

    Spaced Practice   108

    Frameworks   108

    Supporting Performers   115

    Data Delivery   117

    Let Me Elaborate   120

    Distributed Cognition   122

    Augmented Reality   123

    Let's Get Informal   123

    Push Versus Pull   124

    Least Assistance Principle   125

    Zen of Palm   125

    Questions to Ask   126

SECTION III: BRASS TACKS

CHAPTER EIGHT: A PLATFORM TO STAND ON   129

    Principles   129

    Pragmatics   130

    Questions to Ask   132

CHAPTER NINE: MOBILE DESIGN   133

    Analysis   134

    Design Generalities   137

    Design Specifics   143

Get Your Hands Dirty 150

Questions to Ask 151

CHAPTER TEN: THE DEVELOPMENT IT'S NOT ABOUT 153

The Good, the Bad, and the Ugly 153

Delivering Capability 156

Questions to Ask 160

CHAPTER ELEVEN: IMPLEMENTATION AND
EVALUATION 161

Implementation Planning 161

Organizational Change 162

Management and Governance 163

Evaluation 164

We Have Issues Here! 167

Questions to Ask 171

SECTION IV: LOOKING FORWARD

CHAPTER TWELVE: BEING STRATEGIC 175

The Performance Ecosystem 175

eLearning, Strategically 176

Being Opportunistic 178

Questions to Ask 181

CHAPTER THIRTEEN: TRENDS AND DIRECTIONS 183

Mobile Extensions 183

The "Cloud" 184

Impact 185

Sensor Nets 186

Gaming to Go 186

Blurring Boundaries 188
Smart "Push" 188
Slow Learning 190
Meta-Cognitive Mobile 191
Questions to Ask 192

CHAPTER FOURTEEN: GET GOING (MOBILE) **193**
Mobilize! 194

APPENDICES
Bibliography 197
Glossary 199
Tools 203
Checklists 207

About the Author **211**
Index **213**

FIGURES AND TABLES

FIGURES

3.1.	Augmenting Performance	16
3.2.	Media Properties	23
3.3.	Informal Value by Learner Competence	26
4.1.	A PalmOS PDA (with Keyboard)	30
4.2.	A Typical Cell Phone	33
4.3.	An Apple iPod	34
4.4.	An Apple iPhone	36
4.5.	A Nintendo DS	37
4.6.	A Flip Video Camera	40
4.7.	A Convergent Model	41
4.8.	Quinnovation QR Code	45
6.1	Solution Architecture	68
6.2.	Checklist and Description	73
6.3.	Quiz Template	77
7.1.	Content	99
7.2.	Capture	100
7.3.	Compute	101
7.4.	Communicate	101
7.5.	Spaced Practice Effects	109
7.6.	Cognitive Apprenticeship	112
7.7.	Learning Components and Mobile Roles	113
7.8.	Action in the World	115
7.9.	Performer Needs	116
7.10.	Performer Support	116
12.1.	The Performance Ecosystem	176
12.2.	eLearning Strategy	177

12.3.	Learner Performance Ecosystem	178
13.1	Generations of the Web	190
13.2.	Intelligent Learning Architecture	191

TABLES

7.1.	Mobile Category Opportunities	104
7.2.	Category by Formality	105
7.3.	Media Opportunities	120
12.1.	Mobile Opportunities	180

To my mother and father, Esther and Nives Quinn,
for helping me learn what is important in life.

FOREWORD

If you are someone who cares about the future of learning, education, training, and human performance support, then you must read this book.

The promise of connecting learners with information, ideas, and each other has teased its advocates for more than a decade. But in spite of the obvious, self-evident value of using mobile devices in support of learning, *mlearning* has been slow to tip into general practice. The reasons are legitimate, of course. We are still standing on the very early edge of an unavoidable trend that *will* change the way that we think about every facet of learning, education, and training practice.

And yet, it's been hard to shake that prickly sensation that we're still missing the point. Until recently we've mostly, and unavoidably, wrestled with issues of platforms, devices, speeds, and feeds. Finally, we are beginning to seriously confront some of the biggest and thorniest barriers of all:

- Does mlearning really work?

- How do we know this isn't just some pop fad that will fade from view with the introduction of the "next big thing"?

- How must we address the organizational and cultural issues that may stand between the increasingly distributed stakeholders and the learning solutions that they crave?

- How to we ensure that we make it about the learning?

mLearning has been a really, really hard nut to crack. No matter that the apps marketplace has exploded, networks are getting faster, and amazing new devices promise to rock our worlds—the goal of leveraging the amazing capacity of mobility in the service of learning has continued to be elusive.

So it is with much excitement that I share some great news—finally, someone has untied the Gordian knot. I have finally found my mLearning action hero!

Clark Quinn has written the essential "navigator's guide" for charting our respective and multivariate course through these murky, churning seas of epistemology, ontological frameworks, platforms, networks devices, interface design, usability, assessments, outcomes, and ROI.

You may think I am leaning toward poetic prose in tribute to our author, and, of course, you would be correct. But more to the point—for the first time in my memory there is a resource for people like us, we learning tech types who care as much about the learning theory and organizational issues as we do with operating systems and data plans. We now have a framework for exploring the limitless possibilities that mlearning offers. And *that* is something to be excited about.

Lest you think I am overstating the value proposition of a wholistic, integrated framework for mlearning, let me put this into a bit of context. I was fortunate to help take care of the worldwide higher education solutions business at Macromedia in the years just before it was acquired by Adobe. In late 2004 my boss called me into her office to ask me if I would take a strategic assignment. Our senior management wanted to know whether there was a market for mobile learning in education and training. True, it had a lot to do with this thing called Flash. But still.

We dove deep into market research. We did focus groups. We talked with practice leaders. We talked with business leaders. We talked with researchers and analysts. We observed consumer behavior. We observed learner behavior. And time and time again we were confronted with the reality that, until learning and technology experts, business analysts, and learning practitioners were ready to consider *all* of the pieces and parts of the value proposition, mlearning would never live up to its potential.

Some people gave up and moved on to brighter, shinier innovation diversions. But not Clark. He sorted through all the piece parts, filtered out the noise, focused on the things that mattered, tested his assumptions, developed designs, and tested his designs, slogged through the debates and diatribes. And as we fast-forward to today (and I wryly observe that the debate over whether or not the world is ready for Flash on a cell phone still rages on), we all have the opportunity to benefit from Clark's wisdom, vision, and sheer tenacity. He has morphed theoretical knowledge, practical experience, technological acumen, and design sensibilities into a framework that will finally give us all a chance to realize the promises of mlearning.

Clark is, without a doubt my go-to mlearning action hero.

If you are someone who cares about the future of learning, education, training, and human performance support, and you, too, have been searching for *your* mlearning action hero—I'm happy to tell you that the search is over.

Now, get busy and read this book. The world is waiting for us!

Ellen D. Wagner
Senior Analyst and Partner
Sage Road Solutions, LLC

PREFACE

I got into mobile by accident: Marcia Conner (who was kind enough to write the foreword for *Engaging Learning: Designing e-Learning Simulation Games* (my first book) asked me to write an article on mLearning. Not having been involved in mobile learning at the time (though an eager PDA and reluctant cell phone user), I had to make it a thought piece. However, as this was in 2000, it was still one of the first pieces out there, which got me a small amount of notoriety, but more importantly, seeded the thought of mobile learning.

I subsequently had the chance to represent mobile learning on behalf of my client, Knowledge Anywhere, when Judy Brown organized a mobile expo at a conference. As a consequence, I met Judy and David Metcalf, among others, and became involved in running a subsequent day on mobile learning at a conference.

Through Knowledge Anywhere, I was able to get my hands dirty actually developing a mobile learning project that made it into David Metcalf's early book *mLearning: Mobile e-Learning* (2006).

I subsequently was enticed by Steve Wexler into writing a mobile design article for the eLearning Guild's first mobile learning research report. An additional piece made it into the second report, and a companion piece on mobile devices was published by Learning Circuits.

Along the way I have had the opportunity to develop a mobile strategy, offer mobile design workshops, and participate in mobile design activities.

Normally, I would have expected Judy Brown or David Metcalf to be the author of this book, but both have declined. So, recognizing the need, I have taken the opportunity.

Some Clarifications

I use the terms learner, performer, user, and individual relatively interchangeably, although I will try to indicate the perspective I'm taking—formal learning, performance support, usability—by the label used.

I recommend strong use of the glossary for those who find acronyms or terms difficult. I'll define briefly each term as I first use it, but then I'll need to move on.

There are times in the narrative when I use "we" in terms of a solution designed and delivered. When I do, it is a situation in which I was working in conjunction with a team.

I have deliberately included comments from a number of players in the field. This is so that you, the reader, recognize some of the names of the pioneers who have led the way and can look to them for guidance and respect their passion and contributions. All of these people are on Twitter (I am @quinnovator, by the way), and most if not all have blogs (mine is learnlets.com) as well. I highly recommend you follow them if you are looking for valuable insight.

You will see some examples when I do not mention some specific detail, such as the actual organization, for confidentiality reasons. However, I have attempted to provide sufficient context so that you can comprehend the example, even if some details must be hidden. Fingers crossed!

ACKNOWLEDGMENTS

For this, my second book, I have much to be thankful for. First and foremost, for the support of my family: LeAnn, my support system, cheerleader, and best editor; Declan, my fellow writer and device geek; and Erin, my fellow enthusiast and adventurer. I love you with all my heart. Thanks so much!

Mentors Jim Schuyler and Joe Miller, with their vast knowledge and understanding, have separately provided insight down into technical details and up into the broader strategic context of organizational issues. Both also provided the opportunity for roles in mobile development. Partners Charlie Gillette from Knowledge Anywhere and Mohit Bhargava of LearningMate have allowed me to be part of their learning solutions teams, including mobile endeavors.

Many colleagues have been of immense support in this endeavor. My fellow Internet Time Alliance members, Jay Cross, Harold Jarche, Jane Hart, Charles Jennings, and Jon Husband, have developed my understanding of social learning in the broader context of organizational learning, and tolerated my absences. My mobile industry colleagues, Michelle Lentz of Write Technology, Kris Rockwell of Hybrid Learning, Bob Sanregret of Hot Lava Mobile, Robert Gadd of OnPoint Digital, Jeff Tillett and Mark Chrisman of T-Mobile USA, Gina Schreck of Synapse 3Di, and B.J. Schone and Barbara Ludwig of Qualcomm, shared their insights with me. Several worked heroically under short deadlines to provide me with examples. Mobile learning luminaries Judy Brown and David Metcalf not only have helped develop my thinking but were kind enough to share some for the book as well. Ellen Wagner kindly accepted my request to apply her broad industry experience and deep learning knowledge to write the foreword for the book. Gary Woodill of Brandon Hall, who is coming out with this own mobile learning book targeted at the organizational level, graciously shared with me his mLearning design resources. I've co-presented with Richard Clark of NextQuestion, and always learn when we prepare and present.

The editorial team at Pfeiffer have been immensely helpful, including but not limited to the helpful guidance from my acquisitions editor

Matt Davis, the fabulous assistance of Lindsay Morton, production editing of Michael Kay, copy-editing of Rebecca Taff, graphic design by Jeff Puda, and marketing support from Brian Grimm. Byron Schneider synthesized the comments of my four reviewers: Steve Foreman, Inge de Waard, Aaron Silvers, and an anonymous reviewer, each of whom put thought and effort into providing great feedback. I'm indebted to all.

Others, too numerous to mention, have provided aid of some form of another. To all, thanks for all your forbearance. That this book exists at all is testimony to the great potential for contribution in the human spirit.

SECTION

WHY
MLEARNING

Things are moving faster: we have less time, there's more information, we have fewer resources available, and we have more responsibility. In short, the demand is for increased performance. Couple that with the fact that we're more mobile than ever, in meetings, visiting sites and people, at conferences, and we really need portable, personal performance improvement. That's what mLearning (mobile learning) is all about, and consequently, so is this book.

Are we ready for mLearning? The answer is undeniably yes, for four reasons:

- Mobile devices are already here in a big way.

- The opportunity is real.

- The potential is, quite literally, awesome.
- mLearning is doable.

  We will dig into these more deeply in the first two chapters:
- Chapter 1. Is an Overview of why mLearning.
- Chapter 2. Goes into more Details that elaborate on that overview.

CHAPTER

OVERVIEW

mLearning is big already, and is growing bigger at a rapid pace. The time to be thinking mLearning is now!

The numbers are already staggering, and the projections show only increases. For example, the International Telecommunications Union (2010) released research that cell phone numbers are expected to hit over five billion in 2010, after hitting 4.6 billion at the end of 2009. Those are phenomenal growth numbers, and those results are just the phones. Other mobile devices continue their growth as well.

People are already achieving real outcomes through mobile solutions. Industry case studies reveal closer customer relationships, faster solution times, easier tracking, and more. The lists keep growing.

As devices become more powerful, the possibilities for mobile are going to grow even more. It is now possible to deploy solutions across a growing numbers of platforms. And new opportunities continue to pop up.

Finally, the tools are becoming more powerful and easier to use. Providers are making sure that developed content can operate on a wide variety of platforms, and conversion tools mean content already developed can be more widely deployed.

The capabilities that are now appearing are poised to go beyond convenience or small increments and really transform how we learn and how we perform.

Imagine:

- A sales person pulling up the latest details on a (potential) client's situation right before walking in the door, then placing the order while with the customer

- An engineer listening to an audio version of the latest white paper from another group on the way to work

- An account representative using an interactive tool to optimize a customer's contract

- An executive finishing a compliance course on a plane away from the usual distractions

- A field service representative sharing a picture of the situation with a remote colleague to collaborate on a solution

- A learner answering a quiz question at a convenient time

- A procedure being filmed for later review

- Accessing a troubleshooting guide while visiting a remote site with a problem

These are not febrile imaginings, but are happening now. These are only indicative of the wide possibilities on tap for those who are ready to seize the initiative.

What more do you want?

Let us wrap a little more definition around mLearning. The eLearning Guild mobile learning research team, of which I was a member, struggled to come up with a definition. The obvious definition was easy, but there were some gray areas. We ended up with was:

> *"Any activity that allows individuals to be more productive when consuming, interacting with, or creating information, mediated through a compact digital portable device that the individual carries on a regular basis, has reliable connectivity, and fits in a pocket or purse."*
> *(eLearning Guild 360 Mobile Learning Research Report, 2007)*

Let us break that down. A mobile device "allows individuals to be more productive." Not just to learn, but to be more productive. It is not about our personal use of mobile devices, although that's a jumping-off point, but instead it is about systematically leveraging these devices to meet organizational needs. It's about delivering value through the strategic use of mobile technology. That's the topic of this book.

We do that through "consuming, interacting with, or creating information." That's a fairly broad spectrum. How is that different from what we do with a desktop computer? A desktop computer will do that and have "reliable connectivity." However, the mediation is not any digital device, but one that is "compact" and "portable" and "fits in a pocket or purse."

Pay particular attention to this: "that the individual carries on a regular basis." As stipulated, the implication was that this was a device you were familiar with and would be likely to have with you, not only in special circumstances. There are some exceptions to this that I would term mobile learning, but in general I think it is a very worthwhile perspective to consider.

What we are talking about here is not just about mobile devices delivering information to us. That is just the starting point. We're talking about interacting with them, using them to communicate with others, to capture our context and share it, and more. It is quite a large umbrella, but the goal here is to give you some conceptual understandings to get a handle on it to the point at which you can start incorporating mobile into your solutions.

The need to be met is to make individuals optimal performers, regardless of context. We can bring support to wherever needed, and whenever we need to. Meeting the need in the moment is what is on the table, and if we ignore that potential, we may be leaving money on the table, too.

My personal experiences are plentiful, and many revolve around when I travel. For one example, I was visiting back east with a team from overseas assisting me in working with our client. I used my phone to safely navigate from the airport to my hotel and then to the office. I used the calendar to get my confirmation number for my reservations. I looked up the office address in my notes. I was able to use the web browser to find a local store for the overseas team to go computer shopping. While waiting, I was able to check email and have a conversation with a colleague. I found a nearby bank as well when overseas credit cards were creating a problem. And, of course, was able to find restaurants to eat at that met our varied criteria and also snap pictures of my colleagues to take home. This all could be done on the fly, as needed, without advance preparation.

On a more recent trip, I took a new device, a tablet (the iPad) to supplement my smartphone, which I used to write a couple of documents as I traveled across the country. Once there, I used the tablet to present my talk, I took notes in meetings and mind-mapped the keynote, responded to email, tweeted the sessions, and read a book and watched a movie on the way back. This was in addition to the types of activities mentioned immediately above. I haven't taken a laptop on a trip since I bought the tablet to supplement my phone.

Let me be clear up-front, however. Things are still changing so fast that half of any suggested specific solutions would be out-of-date by the time you read this. The good news is that patterns, models, and frameworks have emerged that give us leverage to think about delivering mobile learning independent of any particular devices and tools. And that is what this book is really about—giving you the necessary background to understand and be equipped to take advantage of the mobile revolution. So, off we go. Let's start with the details.

CHAPTER

2

THE DETAILS

Hopefully, you are now ready to dig a bit deeper into the reality of the mobile opportunity. We need to further explore the phenomenal growth in these devices and the fact that real benefits are being seen, suggest the coming opportunities, and provide evidence that there is a serious business case here.

I typically open my mobile learning talks with a small exercise. I ask the audience "How many of you have already purchased a mobile learning device?" Very few hands are raised. I then follow up and say "Let me rephrase the question. How many of you have a cell-phone, iPod, or PDA?" Pretty much everyone raises a hand. "Hello*oo*."

The point of my little exercise is to make the learners recognize just how ubiquitous mobile devices are these days, and that they are *learning* devices. They are *everywhere*!

The growth in ownership of mobile devices represents a technology adoption curve that is unprecedented. As Steve Jobs indicated in his 2007 keynote introducing the iPhone, in 2006 there were more mobile phones sold worldwide than game consoles, digital cameras, MP3 players, and computers, *combined!*

Not only the number of devices, but the use of them is growing. For instance, mobile access of the Internet is growing faster than desktop usage, according to investment adviser Morgan Stanley (2009). Similarly, a report by public relations firm Ruder Finn finds that Americans are spending, on average, 2.7 hours a day on the mobile Internet (2010).

And those folks *are* on the move. The data on work being performed out of the office shows that not only is it already a significant percentage of work, but it is growing. Research firm IDC (2010) estimates that the mobile workforce will pass one billion in 2010. In the United States, they estimate that 72 percent of the workforce is mobile. Yes, they are including those who are mobile some of the time, telecommuting or traveling, but that is a further justification for mobile learning. Not only are there individuals, but whole companies that do not have an office except wherever they are parked with laptop and mobile phone. (And, increasingly, they are able to do a lot without the laptop!)

With this increasing availability and familiarity with mobile devices, people are finding real value. Most of the platform providers, particularly enterprise-focused ones (read: BlackBerry, Windows Mobile) have a plethora of mobile case studies up on their sites touting benefits.

And what is coming is even more amazing. Imagine using a camera to look around you and, laid over the image in the direction you are pointing, are points of interest or businesses you might want to visit. Imagine getting near a place and being able to listen to its local history. Imagine being led on a scavenger hunt around an outdoor art exhibit that not only takes you through the art, but also challenges you in fun ways.

These things are not just science fiction; they are already possible and happening! The tools already exist to systematically integrate data and images in real time, to take in data from the environment and respond, and more. And to do the simple stuff is even easier. Last year my colleague Richard Clark and I conducted a presentation on how to create iPhone applications using free tools for those with development skills that were based in little more than HTML and JavaScript. Even with web pages only, you can start making real contributions.

The point is, the value proposition is real, and the opportunity is already here.

MISCONCEPTIONS

There are many myths about how doable mLearning is. You know: "those tiny screens" and "the keyboard is too small." Let us take care of those up-front.

"We can't provide mobile learning devices"

Understandably, many organizations may be concerned about the responsibility for providing mobile devices. There are several reasonable responses to this. First, as you have seen above, mobile devices are already in the hands of your employees. One approach is making solutions available for their existing devices so you do not need to provide them with new devices.

A second response is that there are reasons to want to provide and control the devices available. Certainly many companies are equipping executives, managers, and/or sales forces with smartphones to provide specific support and ensure communication and access.

"Courses on a phone don't seem like a good idea"

Agreed, but that is not what mLearning is about. Certainly, you can do that, but that is not the real story behind mLearning. As you will see, mLearning is more about performance support and complementing learning, not delivering full courses.

"Those small screens are too limiting"

There is no argument that those small screens are limiting (although visual content is not the only channel we have to use). However, there are two mitigating factors. For one, the screens are steadily getting larger. On some devices, we're now able to not only read text, but also watch movies! More importantly, the amount of information necessary to be useful can be surprisingly small.

"It's too hard/costly to program these things"

It can be hard to program custom applications for mobile devices, but there are several offsetting factors. For one, many times you do not need a custom application, but instead just the ability to access various forms of media. There are simple ways to accomplish that. Further, it is now possible to use nothing essentially more complex than making an interactive web page to make an interactive application. Finally, there are increasing numbers of tools that will allow you to develop interactive applications and deliver on a mobile device. You can spend the resources necessary to create custom applications as well, and you can reap the benefits of more customization, of course, if there is a reasonable business case.

"Mobile learning is all about content"

mLearning *can* be about content, but it is not *all* about content. For one, mLearning can be interactive, not just static. mLearning can also be about communication, connecting the right people together when and where needed. And that "when and where needed" is the *big* opportunity to be had. Helping people when and where they need it is critical.

"mLearning only works when the device is always connected"

While the ability to connect to information sources as needed is a real boon, even offline preparation for access can be beneficial. Devices can be pre-loaded with valuable content that can be accessed as needed. Large amounts of documentation, for instance, can be stored on devices for access. And, as has been demonstrated with the earliest devices, the ability to record calendar events, contact details, take notes, and record tasks to be accomplished is valuable without full access.

"mLearning always has to be interactive"

While interactivity gives significant benefits, even static content can be valuable. As above, having documents available for access, such as troubleshooting and repair manuals or product sheets for quick reference, can make the difference between solving a problem or having to defer until a visit back to the office can be accomplished. Similarly, audio or video files can be valuable ways to present information, such as listening to presentations or watching a procedure.

"mLearning is limited to (smart) phones"

While phones are perhaps the most ubiquitous form of mobile devices these days, many mLearning applications have been made on PDAs, and, of course, media players (think: podcasts) have similarly been shown useful. Certainly, smartphones are increasingly combining the capabilities of other mobile devices and becoming an integrative mobile platform, but they are definitely not the only opportunity for mLearning.

THE BUSINESS CASE

Now that we've taken care of some of the misconceptions, we can and should look at the upside. And there are real reasons to be enthusiastic. The argument is pretty simple: these devices are out there, and they make people more effective *wherever and whenever they are* (not just at their desks). We have already documented some numbers and the growth. We will spend a lot more time talking about making people more effective, but let us characterize it briefly.

As performers, our cognitive architecture is pretty amazing, but it has limitations. Among the phenomena is the fact that we are really good at pattern matching, and we are *really* bad at remembering rote information. Fortunately, digital devices are really good at remembering what they are told and doing something repeatedly. It's about *complementing* our intelligence.

Pragmatically, then, the question becomes: Should it be the learning unit within the organization that takes on the role of designing mobile performance? The answer is yes, because an understanding of how individuals perform, particularly how they perform in areas of uncertainty (collaboration, innovation, and so on), should be the driver in meeting performance needs (the same holds true for social learning, as well). Yes, there are technology issues and business goals, and the learning unit is going to have to partner effectively with other entities within the organization to be effective, but the real issue is providing the necessary support.

This does involve a change in the mindset of the learning unit. It has to move from information provider to performance facilitator. This is an important strategic shift that has to happen in the broader context of the changing competitive landscape for organizations.

Briefly, the increasing amount of change—amount of information, complexity of solutions, and speed of competitive response—means that just executing against prepared plans is no longer sufficient, and continual innovation will be required. Corporations are already recognizing that formal learning can no longer meet the demand, and informal learning and performance support are increasingly part of the solution. The learning unit is critical. And mobile is a channel that assists with all forms of learning.

Just for instance, let us consider some possible numbers:

Let us say that for a sales person, a quick review of the customer's current numbers just before visiting leads to a 3 percent increase in sales and requires ten minutes less work per customer visit. If the sales person is selling $3 million a year, she is increasing sales by almost $100,000 a year on a very conservative estimate. Similarly, if the sales person averages six hundred customer visits a year, she is saving one hundred hours a year.

Now for a field service representative, let us save a trip back to get the right information sheet to repair a device and then a third trip to recover the part needing to be replaced. He can turn three trips into two. Assuming four trips a day, total, he is going to increase the number of fixes per week from six to ten, which when multiplied by the number of weeks, brings fixes from around three hundred to near five hundred per year. While it could be done with a laptop, which would you rather carry, a laptop or a PDA, particularly into a crowded access closet or tunnel?

You can make your own "back of the envelope" estimates for your own organization, workforce, and potential savings. Just think *task by percentage improvement*, and attach dollars or time measures.

Ultimately, the mobile argument is the fact that an augmented individual is a more effective performer, wherever and whenever needed. And that is what drives the business case for mLearning. It is about being optimally productive.

 ## QUESTIONS TO ASK

1. How many mobile employees are you supporting?

2. How widely distributed are mobile devices across your employee population?

3. What are the opportunities for improvement in mobile worker performance?

4. What are the benefits of mobile access to content for the employee population at large?

SECTION

FOUNDATIONS

To really take advantage of mobile, you need some background information in order to comprehend it. We cover this information in the following chapters:

■ Chapter 3. A Brief History of Learning and Cognition reviews how our brains work.

■ Chapter 4. The Technology It's Not About provides an overview of mobile devices.

■ Chapter 5. Getting Contextual looks at mobile learning in various settings.

■ Chapter 6. Getting Concrete provides a number of elaborated examples.

■ Chapter 7. Mobile Models presents a wide variety of ways to conceptualize mLearning.

CHAPTER

3

A BRIEF HISTORY OF LEARNING AND COGNITION

Accessorize your brain!

To talk about mobile learning, we first need to talk about our brains, how we think and how we learn. By and large, mLearning is *not* about learning. At least, it's not about formal learning or, more accurately, serving as a full formal learning solution. We will come back to this point shortly, so bear with me.

Mobile learning is, at core, about *augmentation*. David Metcalf, in his early book *mLearning* (2006), talked about augmentation being a fundamental way to think about mobile learning. Our goal is letting us do what our brains do well and providing support for what our brains *do not* do well. Our brains are very good at pattern matching and reasonably good at executive monitoring, but not so good at performing rote operations. In fact, we pretty reliably make errors: errors of memory and errors of performance. For instance, we do not recall arbitrary bits of information well.

This is an artifact of our cognitive architecture, and we can get around it through brute-force methods, but we have the capability now to not require humans to be automatons. While we can drill information, even then there likely will be occasional errors. The real solution is *not* to try to make our brains do what they do poorly, but instead to support them so that we can let our brains focus on tasks we can perform well (and those that we want to retain for ourselves). We want to augment our pattern-matching and executive function with the capability to do complex but rote processing, exact recollection, and more. We do this already with our desktop and laptop computers, but now we can do so wherever (and whenever) we are. To put it another way, from a problem's point of view, an augmented performer is a far more formidable opponent than an augmented one. (See Figure 3.1.)

This distribution of tasks means we retain the executive function, guiding our performance and exercising our pattern-matching, but leave exact data recording, sensing beyond our capabilities, and

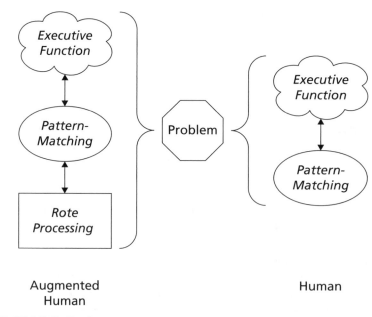

FIGURE 3.1. *Augmenting Performance*

calculation, to devices. Digital devices are the perfect augment. Digital devices can be programmed to "say" or do anything you want and can execute reliably and repeatedly. They will remember arbitrary facts, and respond appropriately to the input you give them—every time. However, they are not particularly good at making decisions or detecting the nuances of a conversation. What we have is a potentially perfect partnership.

So mLearning is *not* about putting e-learning courses on a phone; you should not think about mLearning as delivery of *courses.* mLearning is about *augmenting* our learning—and our performance. This includes a role in formal learning and, occasionally can be the delivery mechanism for a full learning solution, but the real opportunity is augmenting learning and performance, not learning delivery.

To be fair, I also argue that e-learning and courses are also not about learning, but rather that they are about performance. We do not learn for intellectual self-gratification, we learn because we want or need to do something that we cannot do now.

FOR EXAMPLE

Skills

I strongly believe that what will make a difference, going forward, will not be about knowledge, but about cognitive skills. Dan Pink has suggested, in *A Whole New Mind: Why Right-Brainers Will Rule the Future* (2005), that creativity combined with knowledge will be the defining competitive advantage of this new century. Consequently, an ability to continually adapt, to apply more strategic cognitive skills, will be the new enabler. If, as is proposed, the half-life of information is now less than four years, half of what you learn in college is out-of-date by the time you graduate! What, then, do you do?

The new emphasis on so-called "21st Century Skills," skills that transcend particular disciplines, is indicative of two new directions. The first is not to ignore, but to develop learning-to-learn skills, both individual and social learning. This may be the best investment an organization can make.

> The second implication is it will be valuable to focus on a clear separation between what information people need and what skills they need. With mobile device ubiquity, individuals will be able to access what they need when they need it, and what will be critical is equipping performers to be capable of working in an information environment.

Now to refine my earlier statement, while mLearning is not about courses and delivery of formal learning, mLearning really *is* about learning, when you use a *broad* definition of learning. Problem solving, creativity, information access, collaboration, innovation, experimentation, and more are *all* part of learning in my definition. All the information we need to achieve our goals is what mLearning is about: the answers we need, the people we need to communicate with, the just-in-time assistance, the special information relevant to where and when we are, the capture of context to share, and more.

mLearning is really about assisting our ability to *do*! And, increasingly, we're doing on the go, on the run, wherever we are, whenever we need to. Just as we use software on our desktop, so too can software and more be useful wherever and whenever we are.

FOR EXAMPLE

The GPS as Performance Support

A global positioning system (GPS) is a perfect example of performance support. Our task is to drive somewhere, presumably new. Our memory cannot hold all the details of the terrain and roads, so we use a map as external reference. When we have to get somewhere, we access a map, plan it out, and possibly write down the directions. It can be a difficult task, and if we somehow make a mistake, such as being distracted by a conversation or the radio, we are lost until we either can access a map or ask directions.

A somewhat more enabled solution that I previously used was a map tool like Google Maps or MapQuest. I would have it map the directions, and I would print them out (along with maps). With a mobile device, I have been able to access the maps dynamically if I am lost and see whether I can figure out where I am. However, it requires a stop and a manual recalculation. A GPS device simplifies this task significantly.

Using a GPS system, our performance is truly augmented. The system can track where you are, remind you beforehand when a turn is coming, show which way to turn, and recalculate a path if you make a mistake. That is a much richer picture of performance support—having the system keep the large memory information, couple it with routing calculations and attention management—while we perform the complex and innate capabilities of pattern-matching and motor control. This is a metaphor it may be useful to keep in mind during design, as well as an illustration of the concept.

So mobile learning is about performance, but performance as it is seen in the real world. What mobile gives us is two-fold: ways to augment formal learning to make it more effective (coupled with a more enlightened pedagogy) and ways to address informal learning as well (both performance support and social). So mobile can help support the entire learning suite: formal learning, performance support, and social/informal learning. Let us go through those.

FORMAL LEARNING

Let's do a little exercise. Do you have anything you do outside of work: a vocation, hobby, craft, sport, or other avocation? (If you don't, stop reading this right now and go get a life. Come back when you have had a break and some fun.)

Now think about that activity that occupies at least some of your free time. I am willing to bet that you actively learn about that process and augment your performance in multiple ways. You likely talk to other folks, you may read magazines, you participate, try, make mistakes, and learn again.

So, briefly, on my editorial soapbox: *that's not very much like formal learning*! How you learn in the world is *not* like what you see in a classroom. We want to fix that! Okay, off my soapbox.

Frankly, much of our formal learning is not designed very well. It focuses too much on knowledge and not enough on skills, it is not engaging, and it is based on an "event" model (holding a learning event such as a workshop or course) that does not reflect what is best for retention. There are contrary examples, but much of our formal learning fails the "effectiveness" test: it doesn't lead to meaningful and persistent changes in behavior.

Really, the classroom is almost antithetical to natural learning. When you look at natural learning you see the elements that I call the seven C's of learning:

1. *Choose*: We choose what interests us, that which we recognize is important and relevant.

2. *Commit*: Once chosen, we take responsibility for learning; we don't expect someone to teach it to us.

3. *Create*: We build things, we experiment, we try.

4. *Crash*: When we experiment, sometimes we fail, but we learn from those mistakes.

5. *Copy*: We watch others, using them as models, and then mimic their performance.

6. *Converse*: We discuss with others—peers, experts—seeking clues and feedback.

7. *Collaborate*: We don't only work alone, we work with others, creating, problem-solving, and sharing.

Originally, as we sat around campfires in primitive ages, we worked in apprenticeships that naturally had these components. Then we went to master-novice dialogs that were still social, but much more focused on formal knowledge. Finally, the classroom emerged, where we went away from meaningful practice and dialog to a knowledge-dump and recitation format. There are arguments for efficiency, but we can no longer follow an industrial age lack of concern with effectiveness.

The focus on knowledge leads to what we in cognitive science call "inert knowledge": knowledge that can be demonstrated in an artificial situation but when relevant in practice will never even be activated. For example, workplace managers can pass a test showing they understand bullying, and then will go right back to the workplace and continue their inappropriate behavior. And the "event" approach is almost the worst thing you can do if you wish this information to be persistent over time (what we call *retention*). This is a pedagogical problem, not a technology one, but mLearning can serve as a catalyst for better learning. By and large, we can no longer tolerate a large percentage of attrition in our learning. So we need to go back to what is natural to maximize effectiveness.

FOR EXAMPLE

Rethinking Learning

The standard focus on knowledge dump has led to pejorative terms to characterize the experience. Terms like "spray and pray" and "show up and throw up" are indicative of a presentation of content. This fails for several reasons.

A knowledge dump is indicative of a problem in objectives, in the first instance. Subject-matter experts (SMEs) typically no longer have conscious access to how they solve problems and fall back on the knowledge they had to learn. Respectful instructional designers accommodate the expert, and we are off on the wrong foot. Ideally, instructional designers have to take responsibility to ensure the focus is on meaningful skills, not just on knowledge.

A second problem is that, regardless of the objective, too often our learning approach is not matching meaningful assessment to the necessary outcomes. While this can arise from the objectives, it can also be a feature of an outdated pedagogy.

Overall, mobile learning is best executed within an enlightened pedagogy. A culture of learning, a recognition of the larger picture of performance, and a deep understanding of what contributes to learning are not necessary, but preferable for truly implementing technology support, mobile or otherwise.

And just to be clear, our goals for effective learning are two-fold: as mentioned above, we want retention over time until the performance situation occurs; and we want *transfer* to all appropriate (and no inappropriate) situations. That is, we would like what is learned to be available and accessible when an appropriate situation presents itself. And, frankly, most classroom learning events are not optimized for this (almost to the contrary) for a variety of reasons, starting from misplaced objectives through a lack of emotional engagement to inappropriate practice.

When we look at more effective learning, we recognize at a coarse level that we need to:

- Focus on meaningful objectives.

- Hook in the individual's visceral understanding of why this learning experience is important.

- Provide the WIIFM (What's in It for Me).

- Contextualize the learning in the broader picture.

- Use models to guide the performance.

- Reactivate knowledge appropriately.

- Exemplify applying concept to context.

- Annotate the underlying thought processes in the examples.

- Provide a sufficient suite of contexts across examples and practice.

- Ensure practice is appropriately sequenced and scaffolded.

- Align practice with the needed change in performance.

- Space practice effectively.

- Acknowledge the emotional experience.

- Reconnect the learner with the broader context.

There is considerable depth in pedagogy that underlies these points and more, but these are a broad-brush characterization of where much current training goes wrong. And these are *all* places that mLearning can be useful, as you will see, but not the *only* places.

MEDIA PSYCHOLOGY

One of the important aspects of cognition to keep in mind are the relative properties of different media and how our brains process those media, a "media psychology." Using media appropriately is critical not only for designing formal learning but for informal learning as well.

The media we primarily consider are visual and linguistic, but physical dimensions can matter as well (*proprioceptive* information, signals within our body that tell us whether we are upright or not, such as balance and the angles of our joints, can also play a role, but not with mobile devices, at least not yet). Physical feedback gets more interesting, but as yet does not play much of a role. Clearly, non-linguistic audio can also play a role.

The two main dimensions differentiating media are chronological (dynamic or static) and communication modality (visual or linguistic). Within visual, there are two sub-categories: conceptual and contextual. Conceptual conveys abstract relationships, while context conveys the real situation. We can map it out as shown in Figure 3.2.

Conceptually static information can use graphics such as charts and diagrams. Contextually static information can be communicated with photographs. Conceptually dynamic information is typically communicated with an animation, while contextual dynamics are usually communicated with video. Static linguistic communication is typically communicated with text, while dynamic linguistics typically uses audio as speech.

There is an interesting confound with the linguistic category, because it is actually spread across two separate sensory channels. Text

	Static	Dynamic
Contextual	Photo	Video
Conceptual	Graphic	Animation
Linguistic	Text	Speech

FIGURE 3.2. *Media Properties*

uses the visual channel, while speech uses the auditory channel. An additional issue is that there can be meaningful, but not overtly semantic, information, conveyed over these channels as well. Sounds other than speech can be powerful context setters, as can visual cues such as color, shading, and more.

Note that audio and visual sensory channels have separate processing mechanisms, and while there is some overlap, in many instances we can process both in conjunction. Another unique property of audio versus visual is the lack of directionality needed. This facilitates two things: that audio can be listened to regardless of the direction of visual attention and that it can provide information to augment visuals. Audio can draw attention, whereas visual information may not.

In contrast, visual media draws on the rich neural support of the visual system, which can accommodate a large amount of data and convey succinctly a considerable quantity of data.

Consequently, these categories are only rough guides. One medium may be used as an alternative to another: for tasks with high visual load (such as driving), audio can be used. For tasks where it is too noisy (an engine room), visual can be used. Media can also be combined, so text can be laid upon a graphic or photo, and audio can be layered over an animation or a video. Narrated slide shows have been powerful dynamic media (think of Ken Burn's *Civil War*). Nevertheless, having some conceptual rationale for media use helps both use the right media for the task and also considers what potential uses mobile devices might be put to.

BEYOND COGNITION

Even cognitive science recognizes the limits of cognition, and in addition posits two additional components that complete the picture around our thinking: the *affective* and *conative* components. The affective component is who we are as learners, while conative covers our intention to learn. Any consideration of augmenting our capability needs to consider these components as well.

The affective component considers who we are as individuals. While there have been a variety of proposals, personality psychology is working to refine different proposals into a "Big 5" set of traits that define psychological characteristics (Openness, Conscientiousness, Extraversion, Agreeableness, Neuroticism). The question, of course, is what does the affective domain have to offer mobile learning?

While individuals differ, the evidence is that we should develop learning that uses the best principles of learning, not adapting learning to the learner. Research says both that the instruments to assess learning styles and studies that we can and should adapt learning to individual learning styles are flawed. Match the medium to the message, not the learner, is the consensus best answer. Which, increasingly, mobile devices are capable of delivering.

The conative area captures our intention to learn. Do we care? And are we eager or concerned about the experience? While the results on adapting to the learner's individual characteristics are equivocal, not so are the implications of a learner's motivation or anxiety. Let us make it personal: Do you learn better when you are motivated, or apathetic? and Do you learn better when you are confident or when you are anxious?

And these are elements we can do something about. I have talked elsewhere about aligning engagement and education (*Engaging Learning: Designing e-Learning Simulation Games*, 2005), but there are clear ways in which we can and should address reducing anxiety and increasing motivation. Having the level of challenge in practice adapt to the learner is one way, and setting their expectations about what is to come can help manage unexpected and disappointing mismatches. Similarly, ensuring that the importance of the learning, in terms the learner understands and cares about, is addressed is a valuable support for motivation.

In short, our mobile learning, like other learning, should address not only the cognitive, but also the conative elements We can, and should, provide motivational and anxiety-reduction support as well as learning support. We should be hooking the learner in viscerally, making the outcomes relevant, and providing meaningful examples and practice, among other things.

INFORMAL LEARNING

There are times, for a variety of reasons, when we do not need, or cannot count on, formal learning. And, as my colleague Jay Cross, author of *Informal Learning: Rediscovering the Natural Pathways That Inspire Innovation and Performance* (2005) tells us, only 20 percent of what's learned on the job comes from formal learning. We cannot abandon our learners after formal learning. There are many steps to go from being a novice through being a practitioner, to being an

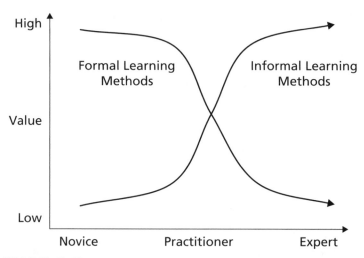

FIGURE 3.3. *Informal Value by Learner Competence*

expert. And the type of support needed is different for each (see Figure 3.3).

At the practitioner level, typically we need less reliance on formal learning. Practitioners know what they need, are aware of the context, and are motivated to learn. They do not need the full wrapping. They may just need the concept and an example, or they may just need an information update. Following the principle of *augmenting* their performance, they may just need a job aid or a decision support tool. There are times when a presentation by an expert is sufficient, regardless of whether the presentation lacks pedagogical elements. The point is, practitioner needs are different than novice needs.

In 1991, Gloria Gery pioneered the concept of Electronic Performance Support Systems (EPSS). The principle was to bring the right information at the point of need in the workflow. Her intention was that even novices could perform sufficiently with such support, and a further goal (essentially unrealized) was that individuals might actually learn through the interaction. This idea is still not practiced enough at the desktop, but characterizes one of the main opportunities with mobile.

The potential support comes back to that notion of augment: having the system remember things or perform tasks that our brains are not good at. By evaluating what performers are doing and what the cognitive barriers are, we have the opportunity to complement performer capabilities.

The opportunity on the table is to optimize our performers in terms of executing against their responsibilities. That can mean making the learning experience more effective or providing support for performers when they are away from their desktops. That is an increasingly common occurrence, as we've seen. We can accommodate time preferences in terms of when people want to access material and context needs, by providing resources at the point of need, pretty much whenever and wherever needed. And that is mLearning in a nutshell.

SOCIAL LEARNING

Informal learning is often considered to be equivalent to social learning, but this is not true. While social learning is a major component of informal learning, there are individual components to informal learning, and there are social components to formal learning.

Social learning informally is the basis of collaboration, and that is increasingly going to be important. As things move faster, including competition, the ability to continually innovate will be critical; and innovation is reliably not individual, contrary to common wisdom. Conversations and teamwork are powerful parts of research, creativity, problem solving, and more.

In addition, social learning provides a powerful adjunct to individual learning. Negotiating shared understanding around concepts and applications requires learners to articulate their understanding and then compare and refine it in partnership with others.

FOR EXAMPLE

mLearning as a Cognitive Augment

We will go into more detail later, but briefly we can characterize the emerging picture of learning augmentation, both for formal learning and for performance support, as follows:

Learning Augment

As a learning augment, there are several major roles for mobile learning:

Adding motivation: Mobile examples can both precede and elaborate on a course and make the need compelling.

Extending learning processes: By providing new concept representations, new contexts of application as examples, more practice, and connecting with feedback, we can make the learning deeper and more effective.

Supporting learner preferences: We can make content such as documents or videos available in the medium and at the time preferred by the learner.

Taking advantage of contextual opportunities: Having specific contexts wherein learning is instantiated, whether locations or times, provides the opportunity to deliver tailored support and consequently more uniquely valuable outcomes.

Performance Augment

Another role is as a performance support augment:

Media capability: The device can represent with screen and audio and capture data completely and accurately with cameras and microphones (whereas our memories are fallible).

Data and processing ability: Mobile devices can transform data and provide computational capabilities that would take a considerable time to perform by hand, such as calculations and decision trees.

Communication: Mobile provides a wide variety of ways for individuals to connect with one another.

 QUESTIONS TO ASK

1. Are you considering more than just courses and including performance support?

2. Is your pedagogy advanced beyond the basic "event" and content presentation learning approach?

3. Do you include social learning as part of your learning solution?

CHAPTER

THE TECHNOLOGY IT'S NOT ABOUT

It's not about the technology (INATT).

—Jay Cross

As we have already established, our focus is on performance outcomes. Mobile devices may be very valuable to us as individuals, but in this context I am talking about real organizational benefits, and that is about outcomes, not devices.

Just to make matters worse, the technology is changing dynamically as we speak. The speed with which new devices are announced seems to increase weekly. The number of announcements that have happened just during the course of writing this book have changed the result.

Yet, we do have to talk technology to have a baseline. This seems doubly hard in light of the aforementioned rapid rate of change, but there are emergent patterns that we can leverage. I will use a brief history of mobile devices to derive an integrative framework that lets us think about mobile devices in the abstract. This gives us a concrete foundation for talking about performance and design in ways that transcend particular devices.

FROM THE CALCULATOR TO THE SMARTPHONE

Although there were some hiccups along the way, including various "luggable" computers and Apple's well-intentioned but ill-fated Newton, the first really viable mobile device was Palm's Pilot. This was the first handheld portable device that truly became an indispensable business tool.

The Palm Pilot

The story behind the development of the Pilot is instructive. Jeff Hawkins, the guiding light behind the Pilot (see Figure 4.1), started carrying around a block of wood in the form-factor he thought would be appropriate. Everywhere he went, he asked himself what would he have this device do to be useful.

As an outcome, he came up with what have emerged as the four core applications of mobile information, tools that allowed you to enter, update, and access:

- Calendar (or Schedule)
- Contacts (or Addresses)
- Notes (or Memos)
- Tasks (or To Dos)

FIGURE 4.1. *A PalmOS PDA (with Keyboard)*

While not all mobile devices have these capabilities (for instance, media players), they define a suite of core capability that is now collectively known as PIM, personal information management. Having your events, addresses, memos, and tasks available all the time became a real performance enhancement for many, myself included.

The Pilot also featured several important characteristics of a mobile device that are critical success factors:

- *Synchronizing* between your desktop and the device

- *Instant-on*, with no lag between button push and a usable device

- *Reliability* so that the device does not crash and lose data

- *Simplicity* in interface so there is not a large learning curve

- *Power* to last throughout a normal day's worth of work

These characteristics are critical for a mobile device to succeed, and they provide the complement to the PIM capabilities that together defined devices that came to be known as the PDA or personal digital assistant. Information you captured out-and-about was automatically added to your desktop information, and vice versa, so you had a coherent environment whether mobile or desk-bound. It synchronized with either your existing desktop environment or its own application, either of which was acceptable. It also happened automatically when connected, or with just the press of a button, rather than requiring any complicated action.

Also, although your desktop was typically on most of the time so you could have access to something without needing to reboot, mobile devices had limited batteries and typically were powered down when not being used (by the user or automatically after a time period of no use). Given that their use was to meet contextual needs, booting up time was problematic, and a short start-up time was critical to adoption. The Pilot came up essentially instantaneously when the on button was pushed and was ready for immediate use.

Further, the occasional crashing and rebooting that people seemed willing to accept for desktop environments was contrary to the need for quick access. The Pilot's software was simple and extremely reliable. The OS allowed applications by others to be available for download, and these were mixed in terms of their stability, but largely they didn't affect the overall device, and the core applications were remarkable in their robustness.

Another factor was ease of use. The big hang-up in previous attempts was either trying to have a keyboard, and losing the associated screen real estate, or trying to do handwriting recognition. The mobile processors, however, really did not have the capacity for sophisticated writing recognition, and the field still is not very advanced. On the other hand, learning an arcane graphic input or using an onscreen keyboard that took up screen space also was problematic. Palm came up with a compromise, Graffiti, a relatively simple-to-learn graphic input language that was close to handwriting, but was unique enough in important ways so that the device could unambiguously determine the characters entered. While not perfect, it was *good enough*.

And while the devices were to be turned off while not used, to continue to be useful they needed to have sufficient power to last through a normal day's use. If the device was not usable for at least half a day, it would not be adopted. Consequently, battery management was critical.

An important feature of PDAs were that most ran an operating system (OS) that allowed new applications to be developed, purchased, loaded, and run. The PDA was a *platform*, not just a device. As a consequence, consumers could customize their devices as far as the imagination of developers and their pocketbooks would allow. Palm soon had a vibrant community of developers providing applications. Microsoft then got into the act with its own OS based on its desktop OS, Windows, and manufacturers developed compliant hardware to create a second market.

Mobile Phones

Mobile phones started out as rather large devices, somewhat smaller than a shoebox, but much more than would fit in a pocket. That rapidly changed, and by the mid-90s mobile phones were indeed quite portable, and the path to today's ubiquitous presence was on its way. Given that the radio technology they use is "cellular," they are also known as cell phones (see Figure 4.2).

With no iconic product helping launch awareness, the practical needs for communication drove the market. In addition to calling, vibrant activity emerged in the area of text messaging. Starting initially overseas, where differences between cell phone service providers were less pronounced and interoperability between systems was better enforced, messaging started becoming popular among the young. I remember a colleague's twenty-something son around 2005 telling me he never used his phone for voice, only for text messages!

FIGURE 4.2. *A Typical Cell Phone*

These days, almost everyone has a mobile phone, and many folks carry two or more. In many cases, people are giving up having a home phone line and just use their cell phones!

Media Players

Another phenomena emerged, that of the media player. While others existed beforehand, the game changer in the space was Apple's iPod (see Figure 4.3). This device, small, with a unique interaction mechanism (the track wheel), and with digital storage capable of holding a staggering amount of songs that could be purchased online or entered from your CD collection, changed the game in online media. This approach trumped the cassette- and CD-based portable music players in capacity, robustness, and size.

While gradually expanded capabilities followed, the real advantages found with the iPod and its ilk has been around the audio capability. As noted above, the peculiar nature of audio is that it is

FIGURE 4.3. *An Apple iPod*

non-directional, which means audio can be processed while the individual is engaged in visual tasks. This provided several valuable use cases. For one, such audio devices provided a mechanism to layer directions on top of a visual task. For another, driving time could be productively used. However, to go beyond broadcast or purchased tapes required another innovation.

That other innovation was the iStore (Apple's software that allowed browsing, purchasing, and downloading music for listening), and then iTunes University (a specifically educational site for finding and downloading audio, specifically speech). This allowed individuals to choose, purchase, and download audio content in the same was as music. One important extension was the ability to subscribe to a source of audio information. Anyone can subscribe to a *feed* (a source of information) of new audio (like a daily newscast) and stay current, using the Real Simple Syndication standard (RSS, which also works for text). These *podcasts* of audio information have become a powerful source of up-to-date information.

Other players followed, playing MP3 (audio) files, MP4 (video), and DVD, but the iPod really marked an inflection point in portable information. The sight of someone with earbuds (small, in-ear head-phones) is ubiquitous these days, whether walking, exercising, or just sitting.

Smartphone

As technology advanced and shrunk, new devices came out that began to combine capabilities. Phones and PDAs got Internet browsers, and media players got PIM capability. However, the real transition was a collision between the PDA and the mobile phone, creating a ubiqui-tously connected platform, largely initiated by Research In Motion's BlackBerry series of email-enabled phones, building upon their legacy of two-way pagers.

PDAs had been limited to being cabled to connect to a computer or using short-distance wireless networks. Mobile phones were able to use the wireless phone system for data that allowed them to con-nect to the Internet in a far wider range of spaces. Connecting these two had both convenience benefits (one of the major drivers mov-ing me from a PDA and a mobile phone was reading an address off the PDA to type into the phone), but also the powerful abil-ity to connect to the Internet. Suddenly, devices could download not applications, but *data* for applications. This was a quantum shift, turn-ing a PDA not only into a device that forethought could equip for use, but that could be reconfigured on the fly and answers found on demand.

Palm managed to successfully graft a phone onto their market-leading PDA, and the Treo was born. As PDAs were still only used by geeks, the sales were not stellar, but the Treo became a treasured device. Only Palm's surprising lack of innovation let others catch and surpass it.

Naturally, Apple redefined the market with its iPhone, an elegant integration of an iPod, phone, and capable PIM running an abbreviated version of its desktop OS and sporting a compelling interface using multi-finger touch gestures. It succeeded despite prognostications to the contrary and some initial shortcomings. As I write this, the market is dynamic, with competitors to the iPhone (see Figure 4.4) appearing almost weekly, but the iPhone's iconic status has allowed it to maintain a market lead.

FIGURE 4.4. *An Apple iPhone*

Handheld Gaming

As a natural evolution beyond dedicated games, little handheld devices that played only one game, the next logical step was the handheld game platform. While other machines preceded it, Nintendo hit the mass market with their Game Boy, and succeeded on the basis of game quality. Leveraging their known brands of games and characters, they created games on a small platform with a screen and controls that mimicked game controllers, not PDA, phone, or laptop interfaces. Competition ensued, and Nintendo released their dual-screen handheld, the DS (see Figure 4.5), and Sony countered with their PlayStation Portable, the PSP.

Educators and researchers saw the potential of these platforms to reach new populations and started developing custom applications despite the technical barriers of programming on these unique devices (unlike PDAs, where simplicity was king, in games the more glitz you can squeeze from the platform the better, and most software development kits or SDKs are designed to give low-level access to the hardware for optimal efficiency and effectiveness). As the competition continued, these platforms started including wireless network connections, media-playing capability, and even cameras.

FIGURE 4.5. *A Nintendo DS*

FOR EXAMPLE

The Leapster

Capitalizing on the concept of a handheld gaming platform, but aimed at the educational market, Joe Miller (at Linden Labs as I write this) led the development of the Leapster for LeapFrog. The Leapster sported an ergonomic design aimed for kids and supported easy development in Flash, leading to a suite of learning titles.

While not initially designed to integrate into the classroom nor support the data collection that characterized Elliot Soloway's work (discussed later), the platform did provide a viable way for parents to provide kids with learning content access in an engaging and portable manner.

Laptop?

One question that continues to bedevil mobile analysts is whether laptops qualify as a mobile device. Recall the definition of mobile learning I cited earlier from the eLearning Guild: "a compact digital portable device that the individual carries on a regular basis, has reliable connectivity, and fits in a pocket or purse." The underpinning idea is that such devices are easy to take with you, so they are *always* with you.

Clearly, anything bigger than a laptop is out. Laptops could be something certain people always carry. Yet, in capability, they are really no different than a desktop. Except that they are, well, mobile, and more specifically, can be capable of doing context-sensitive tasks.

However, smartphones are increasingly blurring the boundary. As their processors get more capable, their software more sophisticated, and their interfaces richer, their capabilities are rivaling those of laptops, and many people are finding smartphones sufficient for many purposes such as checking email, surfing the web, even writing documents or preparing presentations, that used to be the exclusive domain of full-fledged computers. For that reason, the laptop will not be considered a mobile device, although they really are a superset of PDAs in many cases.

Tablets, Netbooks, and eReaders

A subset of the laptop, however, can be considered a mobile device. Tablet computers are typically run with laptop-style processors and sport operating systems that are laptop-scale but with special stylus-capable interfaces instead of standard keyboards. They are also typically both thinner and lighter than laptops. Tablets have been used in medical situations, where doctors carry them around and use the interface to access custom applications for medical information, engineering, and aviation, among other things.

Another take on the tablet is the eReader, which are increasingly prevalent devices. These devices, such as Amazon's Kindle, have been typically focused on providing the ability to read books in a lightweight platform that mimics paper in readability. These devices are increasingly incorporating more capability, however, such as Internet connection and media playing, and this trend will continue. The question is whether eReaders count as a mobile device or not. In their eReader role, I will suggest that they do not, but when and if they are loaded with contextually relevant information or can meet other needs, they qualify as mobile devices.

Netbooks, on the other hand, sport limited processors and memory, with small keyboards and smaller screens than full-sized laptops. They typically run web browsers and are more for using web applications than running local programs.

With these descriptions, it may be hard to countenance why I term tablets as mobile devices, and netbooks as not. The reason is that tablets are being optimized to run applications that are specifically designed for mobile use, whereas netbooks, like laptops, are simply doubling as a way to access desktop-like capability but on the move. Naturally, there are exceptions.

As a demonstration of the dynamics of the mobile market, while I was writing this, Apple announced another potential game-changer, the iPad. A tablet, this device is small enough to carry with youbreak all the time, and yet large and capable enough to bridge the gap between mobile device and laptop. In some ways, the device capabilities are evolutionary, but the device has the potential to be revolutionary in that it incorporates the eReader capability of ebooks, but adds color and interactivity, providing a new level of content interaction. Combined with a digital content marketplace, the device has the potential to reinvent (indeed, resurrect) the publishing industry. And while the iPad is primarily positioned as a content-consumption device, I find the opportunities as a content creation device are more interesting.

Recorders

One other category of mobile devices is worth mention. Digital video and audio recorders have all but made the film camera and tape recorder obsolete. The increasing quality, the storage capacity, the decreasing size, and ease with which files can be uploaded have made the difficulty of dealing with film or tape a hurdle only the most fanatical artists will still contend with.

The ability to capture context, including audio and video, and share with others has been put in the hands of pretty much everyone. Small hand-held video recorders that will automatically load into your computer and up to the web have dropped to the size of a deck of cards and an affordable price. As a consequence, the best known, the Flip (see Figure 4.6), has been put to use in many creative ways for mobile learning.

FIGURE 4.6. *A Flip Video Camera*

Trends

All of these descriptions are current as of the writing, but undoubtedly out-of-date by the time you read this. However, there are trends occurring that give us some indications of where things are going. The short way to characterize the major trend is that things are converging.

Mobile phones got cameras, and then video recording capability. So have smartphones, and recently, hand-held game platforms. Now some iPods have video. Cameras are getting wireless capability. And new capabilities are being added: Global positioning systems (GPS) provide location sensing, accelerometers can react to how the device is moved, compasses know which way the device is facing, gyroscopes can sense more movement, and more. Increasingly, we are getting devices that integrate all these and are beginning to see applications that take advantage of integrating this data to do new and compelling forms of cognitive augmentation. The devices may retain characteristics that indicate their origin or DNA, but they are fundamentally becoming converged devices.

New devices have continued to be released as this book has progressed, and the momentum does not seem to be slowing. Each announcement tends to add new hardware features, such as better screens or cameras or new sensors, and more operating system capabilities, such as multi-tasking or new integration capabilities. The applications that can take advantage of those features then follow. The challenge is, of course, to figure out how to think about the possibilities in a systematic way to provide the foundation for incorporating mobile into your toolset.

THE CONVERGENT MODEL

I believe there's an emergent model that helps characterize mobile devices in a device-independent way. Looking at what is common between PDAs, mobile phones, iPods, and so forth, there are some commonalities that allow us to abstract to a generic representation, a convergent model (see Figure 4.7).

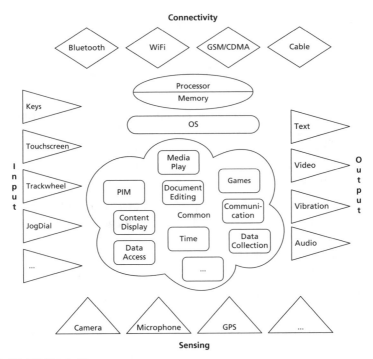

FIGURE 4.7. *A Convergent Model*

The Portable Platform

At core, all these devices are platforms that use a processor coupled with memory running an operating system in a mobile form. There have to be sensors and input devices that allow the device to communicate with the user. And there must be connection capabilities that allow the processor to connect to the rest of the digital world, whether continuously or intermittently.

These devices can differ on a variety of dimensions. They can take a wide variety of form factors, have a variety of different ways to communicate with the digital world and with users, and may incorporate a variety of ways of sensing the non-digital world, but all share the portable processor and communication with the digital world and the user. However, it is worthwhile to understand the scope of variability that can be exhibited in order to help open up the space of possible mobile solutions that might be available and useful.

Output

The first way these devices can differ is how they communicate with the user. Main mechanisms are visual, auditory, and *haptic* (the term for physical feedback). The goal is to communicate to the user information the user is looking for. This can be analog or semantic, and continual or discrete.

- *Screens* are one way devices communicate with users. From limited black-and-white screens, we have moved to screen resolutions that begin to approach those earlier seen on desktops, with color and screen sizes capable of showing movies. Screens tap into our powerful visual processing systems.

- *Projection* is a new capability, where devices not only can present on screen, but can actually beam the image onto a nearby surface, which facilitates sharing the output. While generally personal, mobile devices can be shared (I personally keep diagrams and screenshots on my device to share in problem solving).

- *Lights* are a second way devices can communicate. They can change color, flash, or simply toggle between on and off depending on status. While not a rich media, they can provide information.

- *Speakers* are a way devices can communicate via audio. As mentioned earlier, audio is non-directional and can carry speech as well as sounds.

■ *Earphones* are essentially the same as speakers, but they're private rather than shared.

■ *Vibration* is a relatively new mechanism, but devices can get attention via movement, providing clues about whether something is happening or has happened.

■ *Tactile* is a "touchy" category because, while the manner of conveying state change may seem inconsequential, there are many personal preferences for, say, keyboards that provide tactile and/or auditory feedback. Ted Selker, then of IBM, once demonstrated to me a laptop whose pointing device provided feedback as you rolled over a window boundary. More such feedback may appear in the future.

Input

There are also a variety of ways we can provide input to a device, mostly centered on digital input that in this case means fingers, not binary data. Input typically must communicate selection between options, changing state, or specifying a point along one dimension or two (such as screen location). A variety of devices have evolved to variously support these needs.

■ *Touchscreens* were the earliest form of input on PDAs, although it was often accomplished with a stylus. Advances in sensing and user interface (UI) have allowed fingers to be effectively accurate pointers as well. Note that touchscreens can be several of the following devices, notably buttons, keypads, and keyboards, but representing the layout on the screen.

■ *Buttons* are a simple form of input, signaling a state change or (when held according to a time function, usually with visual feedback) can indicate a point on a continuum. The coupling with visual cues means buttons can also convey different meanings in different contexts (so-called *soft* buttons), unlike fixed buttons with specific purposes (like power buttons).

■ *Keypads* are arrays of buttons for specialized functions. There can be specialized keypads, and there are familiar layouts. For instance, ten-key arrangements can be used for phone numbers or for numeric data (with different layouts, oddly).

- *Keyboards* are keypads specifically for textual input, although often they also support other buttons and keypads.

- *Trackwheels or jogdials* are input devices that use a round wheel (as in the iPod) that can use rotary motion that maps to a continuum of values (so, for instance, rolling left turns down volume, rolling right turns it up).

- *Trackball* is a device that allows one-dimensional and two-dimensional specification. Some also support pushing as a button.

- *Accelerometers* are small instruments that can detect movement, providing a new way for users to communicate to their devices. By shaking or turning a device, users can signal an action. Other sensors are being developed to detect other user-generated changes.

- *Voice* is also sometimes a control option, and voice recognition is becoming more powerful all the time, which can work not only for direct commands, but as a text-entry mechanism as well.

While capabilities in input haven't changed significantly and most changes are liable to be evolutionary instead of revolutionary, the continuing miniaturization of technology and increasing capability of devices means the input possibilities are liable to continue to expand. By being able to communicate with (and through) the devices, we are delivering mobile processing, and consequently augmentation capabilities.

Sensors

Mobile devices do not have to be totally dependent on user input to understand what context they are in. Microcircuits have been developed that can take a wide variety of information from their environment. More interesting possibilities exist in aggregating data across devices.

- *Global positioning system (GPS)* is an approach that triangulates position using a set of orbiting satellites with known locations. Originally used by the military, this system has now been made available for civilian uses. While there are dedicated systems for location, this capability is now being made available in more general mobile devices.

- *Cameras* are now in many mobile devices as well. Capable of still and/or video capture, they can also stream the camera image to the screen, with additional information laid on. There are increasing forms of visual data encoding (see QR Codes, Figure 4.8) that will support attaching device-readable data to the ambient environment, allowing a location to provide information to the user.

FOR EXAMPLE

QR Codes

QR codes are ways that cameras, equipped with the right software, can present information to the user. Similar to barcodes, but with a representation easier to process with a camera instead of a dedicated reader, they can be used to locate information in geographic space. This way, without typing, a user can enter context-specific information into their device.

FIGURE 4.8. *Quinnovation QR Code*

> QR code generators exist that allow the user to enter URLs, phone numbers, a limited amount of text, geo-locations, or even SMS messages, and generate the associated QR code. Such a generator created the QR code shown in Figure 3.8 that holds the URL for Quinnovation.com.

- *Radio frequency identification (RFI)* is a technology that allows devices to read signals from a proximal object (typically, they can be been inserted in animals, or even people). While not widespread, many business uses have been made, such as for inventory.

- *Microphones* allow devices to hear what is available in the environment as ambient information. While now used just for noise removal, other uses are possible.

- *Compass* capabilities allow devices to know which way they are facing. This information can be productively coupled with GPS systems to provide more location data.

- *Accelerometers* can be used not only for input from the user, but potentially can also provide information about the user's movements in the broader context.

The adding of sensors is an area that is still being explored, with a recent announcement of a gyroscope in a new device. Some PDAs had an easy way to add external inputs via hardware sockets, and special ones are being made with specific characteristics for dedicated purposes, but more opportunities will arise. It may be possible to add medical information such as blood pressure or pulse rate measures, weather through air pressure or temperature, and more in the future.

Apps

Applications are run on the mobile processor and support various tasks. Some are built in and viewed as meeting core needs, such as PIM. Others are typically added. Increasingly, so-called *app stores*, online markets that allow purchasing and downloading applications from a variety of developers, have created a broad variety of personalization and customization. It is also becoming easier for a reasonably skilled web designer to create applications.

■ *PIM*, as mentioned before, was the suite of applications initially deemed as core capability. The four major components are notes (or memos), tasks (to dos), contacts (your address book), and a calendar (your schedule).

■ *Media viewers* are core to certain devices, such as media players, but are appearing more generally. This starts with audio and video playback, but includes viewing documents in a few or a variety of common document formats.

■ *Media capture* is also useful, whether audio or video recording or text input. For that matter, it's now possible to draw graphics on devices as well.

■ *Web browsing* is an increasingly frequent capability. Several years ago I heard that 75 percent of cell phones had a browser, and 75 percent of people did not know it. Bob Sanregret, vice president of Hot Lava Mobile, recently noted that there has not been a phone sold in two years that did not have a browser in it.

■ *Communication* is another common capability that applications provide. While phones provide voice and text messaging (SMS), more general devices can often accommodate email and newer forms like instant messaging (IM) in a variety of formats from AOL, MSN, Yahoo, and Skype. Connections to social networking sites are also increasingly being enabled, such as Facebook and LinkedIn. Twitter, crossing the categories of IM and social networking, is also increasingly represented.

■ *Custom applications* are the new opportunity. As developers identify niches and create applications, such as taking advantage of sensors to create new forms of augmentation, it is possible to customize your quiver of tools. For instance, organizations can create their own unique applications as well as custom content, such as tapping into proprietary databases to match up unique information with publicly available information to provide new services.

Networking
While synching with a desktop was a critical step for mobile devices to really succeed, creating a unified information environment, the original mechanism was through a physical cable and so updates were

only possible when the device was next to the computer. However, networking technologies have broadened the reach and started allowing much more complex, and useful, connections between the mobile device and the world. With the Internet available, and the ability to pair almost any piece of hardware with a mobile device, the opportunities become quite heady.

A variety of hardware devices exist to bring data from one machine to another. Universal serial bus (USB) devices can hold data and transfer between machines with an appropriate port. A variety of other formats exist to carry data from one device to another (for example, SD and MicroSD cards). Increasingly, however, there is strong interest in linking machines without physical connections.

Wireless networking technologies range from short distance (1 to 2 meters), sometimes known as *personal area networks* (PAN); through medium area networks (100 to 200 meters), known as *local area networks* (LAN); to *wide area networks* (WAN), which are essentially ubiquitous. Different networking standards are involved.

Personal area networks typically use *Bluetooth*, a network standard that allows two devices to communicate. This can be a mobile device with a laptop or with peripherals (hands-free headsets, for example). This can also support other devices like keyboards, and potentially other forms of input, output, and sensors.

Infrared is another technology that has been applied to certain uses. Using a low-level light source, infrared is a directional standard that offers relatively high bandwidth but only over short distances and the two communicating devices must share a line of sight. For communication, the Infrared Data Association (IrDA) sets standards.

Local area networks are converging on so-called *wi-fi* technologies. The 802.11x standard (where x currently can be b, g, or n; which are protocols for different speeds of transmission) provides a way for an Internet access point to be shared between any devices having the capability. With wi-fi, mobile devices can access other local devices as if they were sharing a wired Internet connection.

While new technologies are coming, the most prevalent way to get data to mobile devices without a wi-fi connection is through phone services. There are two major competing standards: code division multiple access (CDMA) is less ubiquitous, being used in a few countries; while global system for mobile (GSM) is the standard in Europe and much of the rest of the world. In the United States and a few other countries, both are used. While it is not important to know more details than this, it is important to know that in the United States both these two, largely incompatible, systems are in use. This has been a barrier to enjoying the freedom and advances that have been seen in other parts of the world, notably Europe and Japan. Both can provide, via sub-specifications, various levels of data access as well as voice and text messaging (simple messaging system or SMS, and multimedia messaging system or MMS). Subscriber identify module (SIM) cards are purchased and put into an appropriate phone to provide accounts for using the technologies. New standards are emerging that may provide direct Internet connections at distances similar to those achieved with cellular technologies. Just as with the hardware, networking is a dynamic area with ongoing efforts to provide improved access speeds. It is also possible to use voice without the use of the phone services, as Voice over Internet Protocol (VoIP) provides a mechanism for delivering audio across the Internet as a second channel.

COME TOGETHER

Convergence is the name of the game going forward. While MP3 players may get smaller, that is not where things are likely to go. Too small is almost unusable, too.

Instead, it is plausible that devices will stick with a form factor from the size of a cell phone to a small tablet, but increase the capabilities until they are all equipped with a screen, audio, sensors, networking, and input capabilities equivalent to a touchscreen. That is, the smartphone is the near-term endgame, and that is what we want to focus on for designing mobile solutions. Eventually, we will probably go beyond that to capabilities that are embedded in the world around us, so all we may need are a visual and auditory way to present information to us (for example, a heads up display via glasses or a holographic project) and to read our gestures and statements. Our imaginations, not the devices, will be the limit in thinking what else we can do with the amazing capabilities we are seeing.

QUESTIONS TO ASK

1. How can you take advantage of any of the dedicated devices (media player, camera, PDA, phone)?

2. How can you capitalize on the increasing ubiquity of the converged devices?

3. Have you considered the tradeoffs of providing versus supporting devices?

CHAPTER

5

GETTING CONTEXTUAL

Content may be king, but context rules.

Before going into the concepts about designing for mobile learning, it is helpful to review what others have done to take advantage of mobile capabilities. Not only do some learners benefit most from concrete examples, but these anecdotes help illustrate the space of possible application of mobile technologies to meet performance needs and provide the grounding out of which to abstract more general principles.

We will start with formal education, from K12 through higher education, on to corporate uses of mLearning, and then move out into nonformal uses and performance support examples. The goal is not to be comprehensive, but representative, to give you an idea of what is possible with mobile technologies, and to provide some reference points to help complement the more principled treatment of mobile design to follow.

K12

Technology has been slow to penetrate education for a variety of reasons, including cost, teacher skill, infrastructure robustness, and bureaucratic barriers. Technology is expensive, and with decreasing educational funding, money is more likely to go to traditional needs like salaries. The ability of teachers to incorporate technology into lesson plans is, surprisingly, still not well distributed. Schools also need networking capability and support, and these are surprisingly challenging. Also, schools have been concerned about the possibilities of mobile devices being used inappropriately and often ban them. And, finally, administrators have to see the benefit and strategize appropriately to overcome these barriers.

Another barrier, which is not unique to the K12 context, but is particularly a concern due to less-developed skills and responsibility, is the practicality of allowing potentially expensive devices to be taken outside of a well-controlled context. Device costs are decreasing, however, and the benefits are being seen.

One other area of concern is the uses these devices get put to. Already, social networking and communication capabilities have been used in "cyberbullying" and other inappropriate acts. There also exist concerns over the availability of personal data. While these problems are not unique to mobile devices, additional responsibility and education are needed with these new capabilities.

As a consequence, most of the platforms in classrooms are still desktops (or carts full of laptops that are set up as mobile desktops, as opposed to mobile solutions). Despite these barriers, there have been significant initiatives in using mobile for K12 education.

FOR EXAMPLE

Handhelds for K12

Elliot Soloway, a professor at the University of Michigan and a respected researcher in artificial intelligence and education, was one of the first to recognize that PDAs filled an elementary school need that laptops did not. Elliot recognized that laptops were the wrong form-factor for kids' little hands (and had more appealing cost function as well) and started developing software for PDAs that supported taking notes, collecting and sharing data, and more.

With Cathie Norris from the University of North Texas, he pioneered the effective use of handhelds in the classroom. They broke down the walls of the school by incorporating data collection tools that could bring the world into the classroom, and this model still resonates in mobile learning today. For example, portable pH readers connected to PDAs were taken out by kids to measure the quality of their local water. While portable graphic calculators are still in use, the more versatile platforms of PDAs provide greater capability. The barriers still revolve around cost and infrastructure.

Not surprisingly, learning applications soon emerged on these devices as the first mLearning. Newer initiatives continue to take advantage of the mobile form factor, as you will see in the case studies. The simplicity, reliability, and core capabilities that were key to Palm's initial success continue to suggest value in the classroom, and they consequently continue to be areas of focus. We will revisit these when we start talking about design.

From Left Field

Just as in organizational learning, as you will see, K12 education has both particularly contextual applications and some more opportunistic approaches.

One of the ways in which Soloway, and others, have used mobile devices is to take specific advantage of their mobile capabilities and have learners take them out into the field. Whether equipped with sensors for water pH, cameras to read QR codes, or to prompt questions that lead learners around, getting kids out of the classroom is good for several reasons:

- Learners are active, which is healthy.

- Getting out of the classroom is motivating.

- Connecting learning to their local context helps ground the learning in the real world.

Of course, there are consequent problems as well. The needs for technical support now are not localized but roaming around. Management of the learning activity is now similarly distributed, not centralized.

This contextualization of learning can be extended to *service* learning, where learners are actually solving problems in the real world in service of some goal. Mobile devices may be able to play roles as performance support tools as well, such as data gathering via a digital capture application that can then be automatically tabulated and graphed.

A Plot Device

The inherent properties of mobile devices as a communicating processor have been used to mimic more dedicated capabilities. So-called *audience response systems* — where an audience can be polled on questions, handheld devices can be used to register their preferences, and the aggregated responses can be displayed — have been mimicked on general-purpose mobile devices. I recall hearing that an MIT student made such a system work for mobile phones. Of course, whether phones are allowed is a separate issue.

Another way devices have been used is as media capture, whereby students conduct interviews either by audio or video and make their own documentaries or actually create dramas and film them.

Convenience

Graphing calculators have long been used to support mathematics instruction, and problems are designed to explicitly use them. Increasingly, mobile devices can mimic most dedicated hardware, so such capabilities, and others, are now showing up on many devices.

Capabilities that might be valuable include all the usual processing that might be available on a desktop, as the form-factor may be more appropriate for youth, supplemented by any contextual uses outside the classroom. Certainly the ability to take a common device between classrooms is enhanced the more mobile the device is, as long as it supports the necessary capability. I have great hopes that eReaders, at least, will remove the loads my children take to school!

Directions

While the models are not necessarily unique to K12, there are specific adaptations. Interfaces need to be made both simpler in communicative capability for lower cognitive capability and more robust for lower motor control, particularly for elementary students. However, incorporating technology increasingly as part of the toolset available to learners is likely to be a useful adaptation.

It should also be recognized that learner experience with mobile devices is increasing as well. Even at relatively young ages, learners are gaining experience with mobile devices such as handheld game platforms and specific learning handhelds. If this is happening outside the classroom, and not inside, it will increase the irrelevancy of schools for the future of our youth.

There are still barriers, however, and I personally believe we need to accelerate our efforts to help schools look forward. Frankly, in the future most people will have such devices, and the open question is what that means for a curriculum. I will stipulate that the curriculum will have to increasingly focus on learning that takes advantage of digital capabilities, not precludes it.

HIGHER ED

Higher education is not particularly different from organizational uses in many ways. There are some unique uses, however. The particular needs of higher education are increasingly being met through mobile as well as regular methods.

One of the regular characteristics of higher education is the administrative overhead. Learners typically do not schedule the large details of their time, but instead sign up for courses that then impose class times and assignments. Coupled with distance learning requirements, a clear need for course management systems emerged. One of the most obvious ways to use mobile, then, is access to these systems, and those capabilities are emerging. Students can check schedules, syllabi, and assignments online. Of course, this can be true for organizational learning management systems as well.

Other uses of mobile in higher education are less unique. The most systematic and prominent use that has emerged is also tied to the specific format of education systems, in particular the lecture. Particularly due to the rise of distance learning, lectures started to be recorded. The next natural step was to make those recordings available online. Now, lectures are often being recorded and made available as a matter of policy. The iPod and the associated iTunes store for buying music, movies, and television was a success, and consequently the iTunes University for making lectures available was created. Now, many educational podcasts are available through this channel.

Other institutions are using mobile channels. Several universities require having a laptop, and Duke notably experimented with presenting every new student with an iPod (and abandoned it before the organizational inertia was overcome). Abilene Christian University has been a leader in making mobile devices an integral part of the learning experience, providing iPod Touches or iPhones to every student and generating in-class uses, administrative applications, and generic tools like "clicker" (audience response systems) capabilities available.

Experiments continue in universities as faculty members have a vested interest in experimenting with technology as a research activity as well as for their learning duties.

ORGANIZATIONAL

While we will see some case studies in the next section, it is worthwhile to review some common uses already in existence. Mobile tools have been a part of several organizational initiatives to increase productivity.

Federal Express has used handheld devices equipped with barcode scanners for years to manage their deliveries. The propagation of this data through their system means one can track the status of a package almost in real time. Presumably, the cost of providing the devices is more than covered by the reduction in administrative tasks and reductions in errors. This supports performance improvements.

One of the major electronics retailers has similarly used scanners, but in their stores. Staff members can scan the code on any sign accompanying a display and get more data than is available to place in print to inform customers. Sales points and competitive information can also be made available. Workers can use that information when customers are not around to increase their relevant knowledge.

Healthcare organizations are now centralizing their information systems and providing front-line care providers with devices to both enter and access patient data. A specialist provider I saw a few years ago was complaining about how bad the interface was on the tablet the hospital network had provided him. When I saw him more recently, the most glaring problems had been solved and he had become quite comfortable with the device and was a convert to the benefits.

Healthcare has other possibilities that have been explored. A drug trial in Canada used BlackBerries to remind subjects to take their medications, decreasing error rates. Such reminders, coupled with asking questions, can have a big influence in making medicine more effective and consequently reduce costs.

Another way organizations are using mobile is to conduct surveys. It is easy for users or survey takers to answer questions and aggregate the data. Market research conducted this way can be more accurate and timely.

More traditional uses of mobile include providing employees with email-equipped smartphones (such as BlackBerries) or fully integrated Outlook solutions. In these ways, employees can connect with the enterprise-wide contacts, calendars, and communications, having questions answered and collaborating.

NONFORMAL

Other applications have emerged in more nonformal ways. Museums and conferences are just two of the ways mobile devices are being used. These approaches can be co-opted for organizational uses as well, such as premise tours or event communication.

Museums and Tours

Museums have been early adopters of mobile devices. Audio devices, initially cassette players, served as virtual tour guides, and those tasks naturally migrated to MP3 players and iPods.

PDAs also have been recruited to this purpose, providing richer data and triggered by proximity. These devices can also be programmed to provide interactive activities.

Virtual tours have also been developed. iPod tours now exist for many cities, and San Francisco has GPS-triggered narrations for local landmarks integrated with rentable vehicles.

Conferences

Increasingly, we are seeing mobile devices being used to record or to comment on live presentations such as conferences. This has become a valuable mechanism to virtually participate for those unable to attend, and comments have also become a viable backchannel to the presenter.

Conferences now will often have a screen next to the stage or in a prominent main position outside the presentations on which to show the Twitter screen and attendees can track what's happening and what others are saying.

More specialized devices, such as audience response systems, have been useful, but are increasingly being replaced by applications available on more standardized platforms. At the most recent mobile conference I attended, the organizers (the eLearning Guild) arranged for a mobile application that listed speakers, schedule, and sessions. Additional capability included viewing the speaker's slides and tweeting the conference!

THE GLOBAL PERSPECTIVE

At the cutting edge, Japan and Europe have been developing capabilities and using mobile far in advance of the United States. Europe has a more accommodating infrastructure, where it is easy for individuals to move phones from provider to provider. Japan is more technology savvy (some might say gadget-crazy), and cell phones are ubiquitous. Consequently, innovation in usage was driven from these two markets.

Recently, technology advances have started coming from the United States, however, with new OS platforms and integrations. Still, our mix of provider technologies and lack of regulatory restrictions have limited some of the capabilities other countries have seen.

The developing world has been the fastest growth area in cell phone adoption. Cell phones have provided a passage to digital communication that has end-run the traditional paths to the Internet, which are prohibitively expensive. This channel of communication empowering not only new generations, but new populations, with access to the leveling effects of international communication, flattening the world, as Thomas Friedman would have it.

For example, farmers have used text-messaging as a way to get information on crop prices and not be subject to imperfect information from a buyer with a vested interest. This form of performance support can improve quality of life and have a beneficial impact on the developing world.

Sometimes, it must be recognized, digital data (such as Internet-delivered capabilities) is still expensive in some parts of the world, but phone service and SMS are cheap. As a consequence, some enterprising individuals have used voice and SMS to build effective information service. Creativity is key to taking advantage of mobile capability.

Providing SMS or voice lessons is already underway. Downloading applications may be problematic, but another approach is possible. Bob Sanregret discussed an initiative to preload educational software on inexpensive disposable phones, ensuring availability and removing issues of tech support and download costs. One possibility in the works is putting AIDS education on such phones, and basic math or language learning could be very valuable as a way to more broadly raise the education level of the world populace.

Quite simply, the uptake of cell phones is an enabler for a whole new level of access, and there is now an opportunity for much broader access to information. The consequences of access to information is still to be seen, but the potential is huge. The device space is a dynamic area, and change is happening continually. It is hard to predict what will happen, but it is easy to say that big changes will occur. Stay tuned, and consider your opportunities!

 ## QUESTIONS TO ASK

1. What examples of mobile use have you seen that can provide models for what you might try?

2. What barriers do you face in your context, and what possible solutions have others found?

AN INTERVIEW WITH MOBILE LEARNING LEADER JUDY BROWN

Judy Brown is an education technology consultant who retired as the emerging technology analyst in the Office of Learning and Information Technology (OLIT) at the University of Wisconsin System Administration in 2006. In early 2000 she founded the Academic Advanced Distributed Learning (ADL) Co-Lab with the U.S. Department of Defense at the University of Wisconsin System and became involved in e-learning SCORM standards as the executive director of that co-lab. Brown has been involved in technology for learning for more than twenty-five years and with mobile learning since 1996. Since retirement she has worked entirely in the mobile learning area with corporations, schools, and the government. Judy served as a MASIE Fellow for the MASIE Consortium on mobile learning and is a frequent presenter at industry conferences and mobile learning workshops. Currently Judy has returned to ADL on the Immersive Learning Technologies Team. She serves on the Army Education Advisory Committee and coordinates the mlearnopedia.com and cc.mlearnopedia.com sites.

Judy has been leading the charge on mobile for as long as I have been involved in the area. She organized the first mobile learning showcase I participated in, and she has been traveling the globe showing examples and tracking down new ones. I felt it was only appropriate that she should precede Chapter 6 on examples. She was kind enough to let me ask her some questions and share the answers with you.

What got you into mobile learning?

In the early 1990s I followed the Apple Newton, but although it was of interest, it just was not ready. When the Palm was introduced at Demo in 1996, I ordered it immediately and got very excited about the potential for learning with a device that was instant-on, had a long battery life, and was available for use anywhere. I worked with Palm on several Pilot initiatives, as well as with Windows devices when they became available in the early 2000s. Although I promoted the use of portable devices as learning and performance support appliances, it was not until they became connected to the Internet and WiFi that others also became believers.

What have been the interesting developments you've seen since you first became involved in mobile?

As noted, connectivity without being tethered or within a very close range has been the key. Other technologies such as augmented reality, sensors, and location open the potential for so many other opportunities. Most exciting today is the combination of the real world with the virtual world, which has immense potential for learning. It's not about devices, but about the capabilities. It's about the user experience—not the technology.

What do you think is the most interesting trend going?

Innovation and thinking outside the formal course is the most interesting to me. We are finally to the point where we can easily deliver performance support and life-long learning. I am also excited to see that the spacing effects for learning researched for the past one hundred years is now being successfully implemented at low costs.

What do you think people should keep in mind going forward?

Mobile should be an integral part of the learning infrastructure environment and integrated throughout, whether formal classroom learning, online learning, or informal learning. The sweet spots are pre-session preparation, feedback during the formal session, and reach-back following. Start with the needs of the users (learners) and consider the capabilities they carry in their purses or pockets.

CHAPTER

6

GETTING CONCRETE

This chapter presents concrete examples that demonstrate a range of mLearning possibilities and applications. Each example follows a template that indicates:

- The organization: Who was involved?

- The challenge: What was the need?

- Why mobile: What made mobile a solution?

- Making the case: How was the solution presented?

- The solution: What was actually done?

- The benefits: What was expected?

- The results: What was observed?

- Lessons learned: What recommendations come out of this project?

Other than editing for space and clarity, I have tried to keep the content of the examples as they were presented to me.

LEARNING AUGMENT

I found Jeff Tillett through his colleague Mark Chrisman. Both Jeff and Mark are advocates of mobile learning and agents of change within T-Mobile USA. Jeff and I conducted an interview on video, in what turned out to be a fun and wide-ranging conversation. Jeff was kind enough to tell me how they started, with a straightforward performance support application serving as a learning augment that was easy to obtain approval for. This is a great model for an initial application:

Organization Background

"T-Mobile USA is a wireless company and cell phone service provider."

The Challenge

"The primary business challenge is that T-Mobile USA Training and Development is responsible for providing sales training for retail employees and retail partners distributed all over the country. Some of these learners may not have access to T-Mobile USA learning management systems or computers. Beyond training, there also is a need for just-in-time information using devices already available."

Why Mobile?

"Mobile technologies are an obvious option for us because this is our business. Our audience already has devices because of the nature of what we do. This alone can save us significant investment compared to other organizations."

Making the Case

"In order for mobile distributed training to be embraced, it had to be a proven solution. There was also no clear vision of what mobile learning is. We needed to show how easy it was to implement. We also needed to prove that the learners would embrace the use of mobile."

The Solution

"We created some supplemental material and included it as part of a blended learning solution. The training was on a new commission structure for front-line retail employees. It was first suggested that we have a card printed, laminated, and mailed to each store,

Mark Chrisman suggested we could do this electronically and make it available on their mobile devices. At the end of the web-based training module, the students could click on a link and have a reference card with the new commission structure on it sent to their mobile number. The design was very simple and easy to develop. The feedback was extremely positive."

The Benefits

"This solution had many advantages. Print is very expensive and cannot be updated if things change. It also was very easy to deploy. And it required very little development time, just a few hours to create."

The Results

"Based on the success of this first project, we have been asked to do several more with the same approach. It has also opened up opportunities for other types of mobile training and/or supportive content."

PHARMACEUTICAL SALES

Judy Brown ran an ongoing mobile session at a recent eLearning Guild conference, at which I talked about mobile design. Afterward, I found out our presentations and other materials were being made available through CellCast, courtesy of Robert Gadd from OnPoint Digital, as a free service (and, naturally, a demonstration) of their capabilities.

In this example, Robert outlines a relatively common, but valuable, mobile approach for content delivery.

Organization Background

"OnPoint Digital's customer, a leading pharmaceutical company with global operations, was looking to implement a mobile-enabled training platform to support 1,600 sales representatives and professional workers in their Asia Pacific region."

The Challenge

"The proposed mLearning platform was envisioned to support a variety of training tasks, including the delivery and tracking of regularly scheduled, government mandated compliance training (around fifty hours annually with monthly certification assessments) as well as ongoing, group-specific product training, new hire orientation, and other marketing support services. All government mandated training must be fully tracked and reported to the industry monitors on a regular and consistent basis. In addition, access to a series of group-specific training materials and deliverables needed to be prepared, distributed, and tracked on a monthly basis to all field sales teams. Finally, the company wished to provide each mobile worker with ready access to a series of standard deliverables, including current policies and procedures, the company ethics guide, corporate history, and other ongoing business information that all help to shape the knowledge and character of every company associate.

"The key learning objectives sought by the training group included (a) an increase in knowledge retention and overall learning satisfaction for mobile workers, (b) a reduction in content authoring resources and timeframes, (c) overall improvements to the training compliance process, and (d) consolidation of access histories and performance results into one centralized reporting platform."

Why Mobile?

"The key learning drivers are easily tied to the key business drivers for this opportunity, which included revenue enhancement, increased productivity, and system usability. Better training and prepared sales professionals are better equipped to sell more and higher-value products, require less time to travel for centralized training and knowledge reinforcement, and have improved access to just-in-time, mission critical information and resources without having to return to their office or even turn on their laptop computers."

Making the Case

"The company's chief information officer had the vision to lead an effort to adopt a new mobility strategy as part of his larger, ongoing IT initiatives and the recent purchase of new RIM BlackBerry wireless handheld devices for all field sales personnel. Given the fact that all field sales personnel travel extensively and sit idle in a doctor's waiting room or office for an opportunity to detail their latest products and market innovations, the mLearning solution helped to fill that idle time with fast, easy, and secure access to the most updated information on these products, services, and company policies, making the sales teams better informed and more prepared.

"The CIO recognized an opportunity to use the newly purchased BlackBerry devices deployed to every sales professional for more than just standard voice communications and email tasks through a reasonable, incremental investment in a new mobile learning platform that extended the usefulness and accelerated the ROI for their smartphone devices. Group managers also easily bought into the newfound ability to distribute information more rapidly and provide improved performance support at the time of need."

The Solution

"The end-to-end solution is a scalable, enterprise-grade platform that provides secure access to authored mobile content to all field sales teams via their BlackBerry Bold 9000 or Bold 9700 wireless handheld devices. Mobile friendly content is packaged in a variety of different formats, ranging from instructional videos to podcasts to animated/narrated slide presentations to fully interactive training modules and quick reference guides in HTML formats. Content can be assigned and deployed by either training administrators or group managers as needed, and any assignment can also include a short survey or assessment with tracked responses or results. Finally, all content and every application interface are made available in multiple languages as needed.

"For users, the mLearning solution begins with an applet (CellCast Widget) pushed and installed onto each mobile worker's smartphone device, which provides secure access to a centralized content distribution server (CellCast Server) where content is authored, managed, deployed, and tracked. Content authors and administrators create new deliverables using a variety of standard tools and applications including rich media files (for example, marketing videos, recorded testimonials, and podcasts), animated PowerPoint presentations, HTML files, and mobile-friendly courseware built in Adobe Dreamweaver. All source materials are easily imported and converted using automated Wizards that transcode media-based content into all the necessary mobile-ready formats required. From an infrastructure perspective, the CellCast Server is being integrated with other enterprise line-of-business applications, including an internal knowledge base, the corporate LMS platform, and other IT-managed directory services. All content is securely encrypted while on these servers, in transport, and even at rest on every mobile device, ensuring end-to-end security and privacy. The CellCast platform was initially deployed as a hosted service but the organization has the option of moving their instance 'behind the firewall' as future IT requirements evolve or restrictions mandate." (See Figure 6.1.)

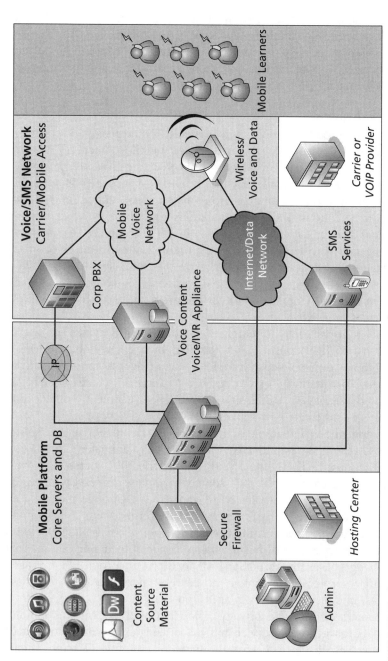

FIGURE 6.1. *Solution Architecture*

"The mLearning solution has been very well received by the mobile learners, organizational managers, and the training and development team, who all find the content easy to access and absorb for anytime/anywhere learning. Moreover, usage statistics suggest mobile workers are accessing their content assignments with greater frequency, meaning they are learning more and receiving more reinforcement when compared with other online/desktop delivery methods."

The Benefits

"Since implementing their mLearning solution, the organization has realized a multitude of benefits, including accelerated compliance reporting, increased worker knowledge, and improved productivity and job satisfaction. Consideration is also being given to the possible elimination of the current centralized online learning portal for compliance testing for all 'mobile workers,' given their newfound ability to access those trainings and assessments from secure handheld devices."

The Results

"Organizational headquarters is now considering how to deploy the mLearning platform around the globe and provide similar support to all operational theaters growing the initiative from 1,600 associates to more than 10,000 mobile workers in ten different languages."

Lessons Learned

1. Even though the organization used leading-edge devices and deployed across major telco markets, all mobile content needed to be optimized for low bandwidth delivery to ensure faster, easier, and more cost-effective delivery through the company's BlackBerry Enterprise Server (BES) platform. *Lesson Learned: In the preparation stage, sufficient time to work with the IT team to establish the proper BES configuration and security settings to enable connectivity, content deployment, and "remote wipe" capabilities.*

2. While most monthly training materials were edited down from long-form content into "byte-sized" learning nuggets, several long-form deliverables were produced, including a 120-page

corporate ethics guidebook, which was actually accessed and revisited on a continuing basis by most mobile workers as a result of its easy-to-read and highly interactive structure. *Lesson Learned: Remain flexible when it comes to content format guidelines; what works for one organization will be very different than what worked for the last one.*

3. Integration between the mLearning platform and other backend systems may be essential to ensuring proper tracking and compliance. *Lesson Learned: Make sure the organization budgets accordingly to complete these integration tasks with all necessary platforms, as the expectation of a full mLearning platform will be similar to those for an LMS in terms of features, tracking, and interoperability.*

FLEXIBLE DELIVERY

I met Kris Rockwell virtually, first as one of a number of tweeters others I knew and respected interacted with (I finally met him face-to-face at a conference). On top of a demonstrable synergy of interests, he was part of a crew that made a distributed game to precede the eLearning Guild's Devlearn 2009 conference. I had been intrigued by his use of a flexible content model approach, and he was kind enough to write it up.

Organizational Background

"Hybrid Learning Systems was formed in 2003 as an eLearning content development group with a specific focus on the development of mobile learning solutions. Over the past seven years, Hybrid has been developing learning solutions for government and aviation related organizations. Hybrid Learning Systems currently employs a team of eight developers and is based in Pittsburgh, Pennsylvania."

The Challenge

"In 2006 Hybrid Learning Systems was invited to respond to a Department of Defense Broad Agency Announcement (BAA) that was asking participants to propose solutions for the automated evaluation of training content and subsequent automatic conversion to a format useable on mobile devices. The resultant content required an XML-based solution that was SCORM-compliant [works with standards for content interoperability] and would run on a variety of mobile devices.

"In 2007 the BAA was cancelled, but our work with an XML-based solution for mobile devices continued. During our research for the BAA proposal, we evaluated the Darwin Information Typed Architecture (DITA) XML specification, which is typically used for technical documentation formatting and delivery. Through our evaluation it became clear to us that DITA would be quite a viable solution for mobile content delivery.

"Our plan, following the BAA, was to develop a system that would deliver just-in-time, task-based reference documents for users in the field. While the exact use case varied—anything from maintenance personnel on a flight line to financial analysts—the goal was to develop a checklist-based system that delivered drill-down functionality and connections to interactive electronic technical manuals (IETM). This system would allow users to quickly access the information they needed and would provide them with as much or as little of that information they required to complete their tasks."

Why Mobile?

"Over the past few years the mobile market has exploded. With current smart devices offering always on, always connected functionality, the delivery of just-in-time training and reference content is a reality. With the development of the iPhone in 2007 and subsequent devices, including the BlackBerry Storm and handsets utilizing the Google Android OS, the smartphone became a much more accessible device that users were relying on in more useful ways. Additionally, the inclusion of wireless network access and the growing presence of 3G networks ensured more reliable data connections and speeds."

Making the Case

"In our situation the case was an internal one. As we continued to evaluate solutions, we needed to find the solution that would work across multiple platforms, offer an open, robust platform, and was light in size. DITA met these requirements and, because it is an XML format, it was platform independent and could be rendered according to the target device. The identification of a simplified task analysis model had already been made and DITA appeared to be the last piece to the puzzle. It was also of note that the DITA specification was moving toward the inclusion of specific learning components that promised to make it a viable tool for eLearning content as well as reference material."

The Solution

"Our solution involved two distinct pieces of software. We developed hybrid. Flow, a web-based system used to develop task analysis documents and output them as DITA documents to be the central piece in the solution. To complement this, we also developed an application for mobile devices called Nomad. The purpose of Nomad is to integrate with hybrid. Flow and act as a rendering engine for the DITA documents that were published. This system gives the users in the field just-in-time access to reference documents that guide them through the steps required to complete a task. Leveraging the DITA format, this information is presented in three distinct layers:

1. A checklist [Figure 6.2] that shows the user the steps required to complete the task.

2. Each item on the checklist can be expanded to get a more complete description of what is involved in the step. This can include graphics, video, or animation.

3. A link back to the IETM for a complete technical reference of that particular step.

"In order to reach multiple platforms (in this case the targets are the iPhone/iPod Touch, Android OS-based devices, and the BlackBerry Storm), we utilized PhoneGap, which is an open source development framework that allows developers to build web-based tools that can access device functionality though application programming interface (API) hooks built into the framework. This meant that we were able to develop the application once and, through some small tweaks, deploy it natively on multiple platforms."

Benefits

"The delivery of task-based instruction allows users to gain access to the information they need when they need it. In utilizing the DITA format we provide a 'write once, render anywhere' functionality whereby the same information can be rendered on a number of devices or as a printed document. The modular format of DITA also lends itself to easy reuse within other content that may be developed. The small, task-based pieces of content were suitable for presentation as short reference pieces to users on mobile devices."

FIGURE 6.2. *Checklist and Description*

The Results

"The program is still ongoing but preliminary results are quite encouraging. Using DITA as a platform for mobile content is proving quite viable as it meshes with existing DITA technical documents and provides a measurable benefit of reusable content. Because the content is XML-based, rendering the information on multiple platforms becomes a trivial matter that can be handled on the server side of the application or, as is the case in this example, by a native application residing on the device. Additionally, the light weight of the DITA specification means that content can easily stream over networks that can be unreliable in different areas."

Lessons Learned

"One of the biggest hurdles when dealing with mobile devices is the sheer number of makes and models that a developer must consider when building applications. Rather than focusing on the application itself, we chose to focus on the content and find a solution that was open and could be easily adapted to a wide range of devices. This approach seems to make more sense when dealing with such a large market. When it did come to deploying a native application for devices, by using a flexible framework such as PhoneGap, we have been able to minimize our development time while providing applications for multiple platforms using a common code base.

"The content itself also shows promise in its format. In conversation with users it became clear that the idea of short, smaller chunks of information was preferable to larger lessons simply due to the fact that they did not want to stare at a small screen for long periods of time. The task-based format seems to work within that constraint while delivering the information the user needs."

MULTIPLATFORM MOBILE SIMULATION/GAME TEMPLATES

David Metcalf, profiled in the accompanying text box, has been creating mobile applications through RWD Technologies and now through the University of Central Florida. He had his team contribute this case study that looks at reusable mobile templates.

Organization Background

"Formed in 2006, the Mixed Emerging Technology Integration Lab (METIL) conducts research toward integration of mobile, games, and virtual worlds for learning. The lab's mission is to further the goals of R&D of emerging technology disciplines for learning and knowledge through partner relationships with world leaders from industry, academia, military, and nonprofit organizations."

Why Mobile?

"Industry statistics on mobile reinforce the notion that handheld is becoming the device of choice throughout our society."

Making the Case

"In many cases, learning populations are already using mobile devices for other activities, such as customer relationship management (CRM) or in daily use for mobile messaging/communications. In these situations, our primary approach is to evaluate opportunities regarding how to best leverage the existing investment of the technology and integrate its use into the science of learning and performance. Additionally, we focus on identifying areas of quick wins."

Common Learning Objectives

- "Increase learner access to (or sharing of) information by making it widely available and easily accessible.

- Break through the clutter of email and other types of digital communications by providing learners with targeted, tightly focused content messages.

- Raise learner retention and application of content.

- Improve training efficiency and business impact by decreasing the cost of training per learner, both in training costs as well as employee time off task.

- Allow for the integration of appropriate learning theories within existing training programs.

- Implement, test, and record the impact of learning mashup theories.

- Ensure the approach to convert existing web course into mobile compatible courses is consistent with the internal guidelines for content presentation, navigation, media, code, and style.

- Create mashups of internal suites of software applications with mobile courses.

- Provide delivery alternatives to accommodate different wireless plans.

- Enhance existing learning and support models by expanding reach of knowledge objects to handheld devices; create new objects when necessary."

The Challenge

"The company's suite of existing desktop-based learning courses (internal content) were not compatible with handheld devices. The organization was unsure how to optimize the retrofitting/redesign of said content into format for mobile. Additionally, this organization faced an instructional system design model in transforming these aforementioned mobile courses into performance support modules and audio materials to complement existing internal sales and marketing initiatives."

The Solution

"The solution was developed to leverage the mobile web, instead of a platform-specific application. This made the solution viable across any device that could access the web. The program also made use of animated gifs to display images, instead of Flash, as well as HTML5. Since some phones cannot run Flash, this further increased accessibility across multiple devices, in addition to reducing the bandwidth and processing power required. The program itself was adjusted and edited to work with various mobile web browsers, as each browser interprets code in slightly different ways and might recognize images and formatting differently. Formatted to fit a mobile phone's small web browser, the game was golf themed and each question a player attempted represented a shot on the current hole. The game was driven by simple, button-based menus, and players were awarded points based on their answers and overall performance." (See Figure 6.3.)

Lessons Learned

"The primary lesson learned from this project was the usefulness of mobile web-based programs over applications written for a specific platform. This program could be made available to a much broader audience and was extremely easy to access online. While this is not the case for every solution to every challenge, deciding whether a solution should be developed using the mobile web or as an application is an important consideration."

ADDRESSING STEM VIA MOBILE

Bob Sanregret connected me to Heather A. Katz, Ph.D., currently with Personnel Decisions Research Institute, who was part of a project developing a mobile education initiative using OutStart's Hot Lava Mobile solution.

This initiative focuses on upper elementary through high school, augmenting more formal education, and consequently explores different facets of mobile education. Heather was kind enough to share the case study with us.

Organization Background

"This case study examined a project produced through a partnership between the Ewing Marion Kauffman Foundation and Hot Lava Software, Inc. The Kauffman Foundation is the world's largest

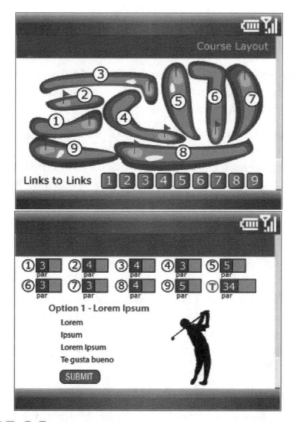

FIGURE 6.3. *Quiz Template*

foundation devoted to entrepreneurship with a focus that is two-fold: advancing entrepreneurship and improving the education of children and youth."

The Challenge

"The two-phased study involved delivering and evaluating science, technology, engineering, and mathematics (STEM) education via mobile phones. Three main goals of the project (participation, change agency, and inspiration) directed the following hypotheses:

1. Mobile phones are a viable medium to globally engage learners with science, technology, engineering, and mathematics (STEM) education.

2. STEM education delivered via mobile phones can serve as a change agent example to influence other entities to deliver education via mobile devices.

3. Youth are inspired by relevant content (that is, sports-based content) and respected role models (professional athletes) to engage with STEM via mobile phones.

"The main learning objective was to raise youth's awareness and knowledge of STEM theories and concepts. The pedagogical design involved context-based instructional materials (sports-themed STEM content) delivered via mobile devices to connect real-world events (sporting events) with STEM concepts. Sports Bytes™ (primarily focusing on soccer and baseball) are sports-themed STEM educational modules—brainteaser content and quick quizzes."

Why Mobile?

"Mobile technologies provide a venue for informal learning that occurs anywhere, any place and relates to authentic real-world activities. The project design was grounded in the understanding that students learn better when they relate STEM to real-world experiences and that STEM knowledge can improve by applying mobile learning to the solution of authentic problems."

Making the Case

"Fortunately, there was no need to convince the Kauffman Foundation. They sought a mobile approach, and the project was fully funded by the Kauffman Foundation. However, the key to securing user participation was implementing an incentive program. Users could win an iPod or a baseball stadium prize pack for their participation in answering at least one Sports Bytes question via their mobile device."

The Solution

"The solution was delivered (both SMS and browser-based) via mobile phones. Phase I results included 16,362 registered users, of which 10,532 qualified users from over 114 countries answered at least one question. Phase II results included 398, 919 registered users from over 116 countries, of which 104,041 qualified users answered at least one question via a browser.

"In Phase I, the mobile content was designed using a more traditional instructional systems design strategy—presenting the learner with the learning objectives and instructional content first, followed by a knowledge assessment. However, this unintentionally deterred users from cognitively engaging with the STEM content. User observation trials involving learners 'thinking-aloud' indicated that users wanted to view a question along with response choices, enter their response, and then receive a few sentences that explained the correct response. Hence, in Phase I users were redirected to the question; bypassing the instructional front matter users could freely navigate back to the instructional content. In Phase II, Sports Bytes was redesigned to first present the user with a brainteaser question and accompanying response choices. In both phases, upon entering a response choice the learner was presented with the correct answer accompanied by explanatory instructional text. There were three levels of difficulty: Level I: Beginner (fifth and sixth grade), Level II: Intermediate (middle school), and Level III: Advanced (high school)."

Deployment

"Hot Lava's Mobile Delivery and Tracking System (MDTS) was used to deliver content via mobile phones and track users' participation using WAP 2.0 services.

"Participation was solicited through paid advertising and mobile content portals. Baseball stadium participation was also encouraged through message boards. Sports Bytes content was guided by two theoretical frameworks: integrated thematic (Kovalik, 2001) and authentic instruction (Newman & Wehlage, 1993) associating STEM concepts with popular sports (baseball, soccer, swimming, cycling, and table tennis). Patten, Sánchez, and Tangney's (2006) framework provided an *interactive* and *location aware* design to the content including input and output capabilities of the mobile device. A Sports Bytes user could not only answer a brainteaser question but also receive feedback in the format of the answer with an instructional explanation, supporting learning. Location awareness was provided by making connections to the sporting event and public display of user responses."

The Benefits

"Sports Bytes provided an enhanced cognitive environment in which mobile learners interacted with STEM content, their physical and mobile environments, and each other. The ability to instantly access informal learning in real world contexts through mobile devices that result in recorded and published responses can empower users to become investigators and active learners who are responsible for their own knowledge acquisition and decision making."

The Results

1. "Mobile phones are a viable medium to globally engage learners with science, technology, engineering, and mathematics (STEM) education. This hypothesis was realized as indicated by exceeding participation goals: 415,281 registered users accessed Sports Bytes, and 114,573 qualified users answered at least one question.

2. STEM education delivered via mobile phones can serve as a change agent example to influence other entities to deliver education via mobile devices. This hypothesis was also proven true in successful applications by other organizations, including the Kauffman Foundation (introducing the Voyage Exhibition with fifteen SMS quizzes); kajeet's™ continued hosting of Sports Bytes; For Inspiration and Recognition of Science and Technology (FIRST) provided relevant quizzes via their cell phones to test their knowledge about robots at the event; The Junior Engineering Technical Society development of JETS Bytes; and, a major U.S. telecom service provider entered into an agreement with Kauffman to host Sports Bytes on their phone deck.

3. Youth are inspired by relevant content (sports-based content) and respected role models (professional athletes) to engage with STEM via mobile phones. This hypothesis was proven true when during Phase II, 104,041 qualified users cumulatively yielded 648,970 responses from forty questions."

Lessons Learned

"It is recommended that mLearning projects must:

■ Analyze users, their tasks, and their environments, including the range of places and times the device may be used and the possible atmospheric conditions, lighting, and noise levels.

■ Test new mLearning content with real users in their respective learning communities prior to implementation.

■ Ensure that the haptic characteristics of the device do not negatively affect the users' ability to successfully use the device or their ability to interact comfortably with the mLearning content.

▪ Additionally, providing information and instruction in the manner that will motivate users to engage with the content is critical for learner interaction."

References

Kovalik, S. (2001). *Exceeding expectations: A user's guide to implementing brain research in the classroom.* Black Diamond, WA: Books for Educators.

Newman, F.M., & Wehlage, G. (1993). Five standards of authentic instruction. *Educational Leadership, 7*.

Patten, B., Sánchez, A. I., & Tangney, I. (2006). Designing collaborative, constructionist and contextual applications for handheld devices. *Computers & Education, 46*(3), 294–308.

MAKING MOBILE AT ST. MARYS

Scott Newcomb reached out to me about mobile and happily contributed this story of how their school district is using mobile to deliver more effective and efficient learning.

Organization Background

"St. Marys City Schools (SMCS) has an enrollment of 2100+ students in grades K through 12. The city of St. Marys is located in Western Ohio. St. Marys has five school buildings located throughout the district. St. Marys Primary School hosts grades PK to 2; St. Marys Intermediate School hosts grades 3 to 5; St. Marys Middle School hosts grades 6 to 8, and St. Marys Memorial High School hosts grades 9 to 12."

The Challenge

"SMCS has limited space for multiple computer labs throughout the district. There are two computer labs located in the St. Marys Intermediate School for grades 3 to 5. Due to the building project, the district was limited in updating and purchasing computers for classrooms and computer labs. The age of the computers ranged from three years up to nine years old. There were three different operating systems (Windows 98, Windows 2000, and Windows XP). There were three different versions of Microsoft Office (Office 2000, Office 2003, and Office XP). SMCS Technology Department was looking for a solution where all of the students can work on the most recent technology with the most recent software at a minimal cost. The smartphones (mobile learning devices—MLD) made the most sense due to facility space and mobility.

"With the MLD the teachers were able to cover more material in a shorter time frame. With the computer labs, the teachers had to sign up to use them. Many times the computer labs were already reserved for other teachers. The labs were booked days or weeks in advance. By the time the computer labs were available, the assignment was too late to do. With the MLDs, the teachers can work on activities right away. With simple word processing activities, the teachers felt like the students were writing more because the word processing was much quicker to correct or edit. The students were able to make changes much quicker and allowed for more writing to occur. With the mobile technology, the teachers are able to give more practice activities and lessons."

Why Mobile?

"Classroom space is limited. The MLDs allow the students to do work at their desks. A small area is provided where the students charge the devices. The students can take the devices on field trips to take pictures, record videos, take notes, and create audio files. SMCS has created a classroom without walls.

"The students are used to playing with handheld devices. As educators, we tell students to put away those devices and come to school and work on computers that are outdated. The students' world revolves around mobility and mobile devices. We as teachers were not preparing the students for the future. We were not meeting their needs and their demands. In two years of implementing mobile learning devices in the classroom, we have seen an increase in critical thinking skills, communication skills, collaboration building skills, and creativity/innovation skills. The teachers are able to create differentiated learning activities and all students of various learning levels can be intermingled within the same classroom."

Making the Case

"SMCS started out with a pilot project of two third-grade teachers, two fourth-grade teachers, two fifth-grade teachers, two resource teachers, an elementary building principal, and the technology coordinator. The school district purchased sixty PDAs, sixty GoKnow application software licenses, sixty protective cases, and sixty wireless keyboards. The total cost for the first year was approximately $44,000. The money came from the general fund. The first two classes that used the devices were so excited after using the PDAs one week that the local VFW donated money, the parent teacher organization donated money, and the principal's fund donated money. Toward the end of the project in year one, many parents were requesting teachers who would be using the devices in year two. Many parents commented on how positive their children were about school. They enjoyed coming to school and learning with the MLDs. In year two, the district used general fund money as well as stimulus grant money to equip all third through sixth grade students and staff.

"The most important element to securing sponsorship for the project is a tie between student enthusiasm, teacher enthusiasm, parent excitement, and administration excitement. All four elements were very important in moving forward to implementing grades three through six in year two of the project. SMCS have created a positive learning environment for all students and teachers (640+ users) by implementing the MLDs in the classroom."

The Solution

"SMCS is using a learning management system called GoKnow Learning software. The software has applications that work within the scope of the program. The teachers have the ability to log into the system and create a paperless environment. They are able to create activities/assignments/lessons and send the them electronically to the students' MLDs.

"The GoKnow software was loaded on a microSD card and installed on all MLDs. Once the software was installed, any updates or additional software installed on the device could be done by syncing the devices electronically. From a technology department standpoint, the software is installed very quickly and the students can help load new software applications with minimal technology support.

"The students truly enjoy using the various software applications installed on the MLDs. The students are given the freedom to customize the device however they want. SMCS talks about proper MLD etiquette. An acceptable user policy was developed for the students so that they understand the consequences if the MLD is misused."

The Benefits

"SMCS makes monthly payments to pay for the broadband Internet cost. The school district was able to obtain the MLDs free of charge due to government pricing. The district doesn't have to spend lots of up-front money to purchase the broadband service compared to purchasing laptops or netbooks. With the use of MLDs, SMCS is charged for devices that are activated. If a device doesn't work, SMCS disables the service for the broken device and activates a new device. The downtime is minimal compared to a broken laptop, netbook, or desktop computer. The district would have to purchase additional netbooks, laptops, or computers as spares to replace units that aren't working correctly. Every year, SMCS will receive new MLDs at no cost with the latest updated software.

"The cost of broadband Internet has continually dropped over the past four years. Competition is becoming very strong between the cell phone companies, which is driving the cost down, making it more affordable for schools to implement this type of technology. The broadband Internet qualifies for E-rate discounts, which will lower the cost even more for poor school districts. St. Marys receives 61 percent E-rate discounts on Internet services, long distance services, and local phone services. SMCS pays $9.75 per month instead of the regular $25 per month. This is a significant savings for the district. SMCS uses the MLDs for the school year only, which is nine months. The cost to use the device for each child is $87.75 per school year. The software costs $25 per year. The total cost for each student for broadband and software is $112.75."

The Results

"Students who used the devices last year showed improvements on the state achievement tests. The fourth-grade students showed an 11 point improvement in math. Teachers have said that the students' writing assignments have improved by using the mobile technology in the classroom. The students are asking if they can write more. Through teacher observations, the students are more engaged. The students look for new ways to use the MLDs in daily class work. The teachers have seen changes in student behavior and credit the MLD for bringing about the changes."

Lessons Learned

"A key factor is to start out with a small group of teachers who want to try something new and aren't afraid of working with the students and the devices. Regular professional development training is very important in working with staff members. The staff members need co-workers they can depend on to help in a pinch. The teachers need to allow the students to explore and run with the project. The project coordinator needs to keep the administration, board of education, and parents involved with the project. When first starting the project, the teachers should have a meeting with the parents to explain how the project is going to work. Try to get the media involved so that the community can follow along with the project as well. The project manager needs to go to various community service organizations and talk about the project and invite community members into the classrooms to see the students in action. The students are the best sellers of the project."

LEARNING WWW (WHEREVER WHENEVER AND WHATEVER)

I met Gina Schreck, president and digital immigration officer for Synapse 3Di, at a conference, and then heard her speak. Highly engaging as a presenter and in person, she has seemingly endless energy.

Among her compelling tales of using new media to meet organizational learning needs was one about using mobile video cameras, illustrating an upcoming model for mobile. She was kind enough to write it up.

Organization

"Service Magic was founded in 1998 in Golden, Colorado, providing prescreened and customer-rated contractors and home service professionals. In July 2004, IAC/InterActiveCorp acquired Service Magic and they joined LendingTree, HSN, Evite, Citysearch, Ask Jeeves, and a host of other interactive companies. Service Magic currently employs a little over one thousand employees, with over five hundred of them in the sales team."

The Challenge

"In late 2008, the sales team had a learning management system that no one seemed to be using. The online courses were filled with lots of text and static screen shots. Managers said they didn't have time, and many said the programs were boring. Learning content was loaded on the company intranet and handouts were given to each team member to use as reference material when speaking to customers. The material was put into a binder and rarely looked at again. Managers were supposed to have their team members log on and take tests to measure their comprehension of learning materials. It wasn't happening. We looked at the reports and found that six people (out of 350 sales people) had actually used the program in the past quarter. The quality assurance team listens to phone calls and measures each rep on several key factors, one being accuracy of information given. The accuracy rate was dipping below 50 percent."

Why Mobile?

"The environment at Service Magic is an extremely fast-paced call center. They have centers in Golden, Colorado, and Kansas City, Kansas. Managers have limited time to spend in traditional training classes and had a list of reasons why they could not make traditional classroom training work for them. Individual coaching and on-the-spot training is ideal, but the managers did not have enough content to be delivered consistently. The population is fairly young at Service Magic (average age in sales team is thirty) and tech-savvy. Most are active on social media sites and listen to music on iPods or other MP3 players. The sales teams are made up of commissioned sales people and they do not want to be off the phones."

Making the Case

"It was not hard at all to propose new and creative solutions to their learning challenges. Because what they currently had was not being used, and obviously not working, they were open to trying new ideas and the pieces that we started with were very easy to play with and experiment."

The Solution

"We used a multi-layered approach and got as many people involved in co-creating content as we could enlist. Our goal was to create a 'LEARNING in BYTE-SIZED PIECES' campaign filled with fun videos created by the learners themselves. There was a new product being rolled out so the contest was announced at an all-hands meeting. Each sales team was tasked with creating a three-to-five-minute video explaining the new product. Their videos would be judged on creativity and content. The teams were given one Flip video camera per team, and the contest was on. Content was loaded on the intranet on the company's Facebook fan page, and materials were printed and given to each team member to use in their research. Two weeks later there was a 'Movie Premier' that took place all day. The videos were shown several times throughout the day with popcorn provided. The teams were extremely creative and actually researched the information that was posted on the intranet to be sure their content was correct. The videos were shared with other departments, and the learning spread beyond the sales team. We asked participants to share what they learned and how they will apply the information. This was captured on video as well and shared with upper management. The enthusiasm and buzz was so great that immediately one of the sales team members suggested they send cameras out to some of their customers to create a customer service training campaign. 'A Day in the Life of a Service Magic Customer' was the next 'movie day' learning event.

"We loaded MP3 players with coaching modules and audio books for anyone to check out like a library. Each manager created a ten-minute learning-cast to share best coaching stories. These were placed in a 'Managers' Library' for download. A virtual book club was started with the sales management team and to include the Kansas City managers, they used the Synapse 3Di campus in Second Life for their monthly book club meetings. With the guidance of their director and a coach/facilitator, they logged in and discussed the concepts in that month's particular business book and together committed to implementing two or three of the points. They would report back the next month what they discovered, what the challenges were, and how to adjust the approach for success.

"We have since combined several other 'pieces' to the mobile approach. New hires are given a different color lanyard for their badges for the first three months so they can be identified easily on the sales floor. Experienced reps and managers are encouraged to stop and share things they know now that have helped them on their job. The new reps track who shared what and those who are sharing are recognized in weekly meetings.

"The Hybrid Program was created to allow team members to spend a day shadowing an employee from another department once a quarter. They create a ten-minute presentation from what they learned and share that at the weekly team meetings.

"Their training manager has now hired an 'innovation coordinator' who is tasked with creating new ways to deliver learning content."

The Benefits and Results

"Employees not only have started looking forward to new learning campaigns, but they are submitting ideas and ways to teach each other. The learning department has shifted from managing a system to co-creating content with team members. When mystery calls were made and the quality assurance team monitored calls, they found the accuracy rate of information shared with customers is now steadily over 70 percent."

Lessons Learned

"We learned that participants do want to learn new information, but they LOVE participating in the creation of that content. Through podcasts and video, the learners are now excited to become teachers. Other departments are now incorporating these techniques to learn and teach. The advice this team is now giving to other departments and other companies is to break the mold, start from scratch, and let the learners get involved in teaching. Nothing makes learners learn deeper than knowing they have to teach the content, and if they can have fun doing it, they can't wait for the next opportunity!"

UBIQUITOUS GAMES

Jim "Sky" Schuyler, CEO of Red7 and Cyberspark.net, hired me for my first real job out of college, designing and programming educational computer games at DesignWare (which eventually led to my *first* book), and then again bringing me back to the United States to lead a team developing an intelligently adaptive learning system for Knowledge Universe Interactive Studio. He has been doing learning technology (and more) since the days of Pilot and Plato, and has served as mentor, colleague, and friend.

Early on, Sky saw the vision of a ubiquitous learning experience and developed an architecture to deliver it. This example illustrates the development of his far-reaching approach. Despite being involved in bits and pieces of it, I asked him to lay out the thinking behind it and some of the applications.

Organization Background

"Red7 is dedicated to facilitating communication by building software and network technologies. In 2002, at Red7, Sky began combining his understanding of software and tech to start building real-world *mixed-reality* experiences."

The Challenge

"My idea was to have a central computer/server that would utilize a *scenario* to determine which medium, and what message, to send to each player at the appropriate time. And players would react to those messages, perhaps through a different medium. In order to react, they'd have to learn how to use some function (like setting up a voicemail greeting, for instance).

"A player would join the game when invited (like the movie *The Game*). Invitations might be sent by email, or made by phone, with the computer calling the shots. The players would react by replying to the email or calling a phone number, and would receive the first task or challenge. They would then go off and try to accomplish the task or solve the challenge, and then reply back to the game in the required fashion (again, this was usually email). The *scenario* was a set of rules that told the computer what to do as the player responded to each question, task, or challenge. In effect, it was only about as intelligent as a simple computer-based learning program, but the tasks the learner was carrying out could be vastly more complex, and there could be a considerable time between the asking of the question and the giving of the answer or solution!

"It became obvious pretty quickly that a *scenario* could be very sophisticated if combined with the right media. It could go way beyond simple programmed instruction, and since it incorporated real-world processes, it could involve some pretty sophisticated learning processes 'between' the question and the eventual answer.

"Our first attempt at a real scenario was a sales simulation. We incorporated email, phone, the company intranet, and the company's own sales process. The targeted behavior was to get the telephone sales representatives to respond to inquiries by sending back the appropriate product information. Reps were 'enrolled' in the game with their knowledge, but not knowing what kind of questions they would receive or when they'd receive them. Within a day, several emails would arrive (sent by the *scenario* or course) with inquiries about what product was the right one for particular needs. The sales person wouldn't be able to tell (at least initially) whether these inquiries were real people or simulated people. The rep was to determine what information to send back, and in one case the inquiry gave a phone number, which the rep could call. The phone number was a voicemail number with a message about a specific product need (at this point it became obvious to the rep that this was the training scenario), and the rep had to send the correct information to an in-game email address. If the proper information was sent, the scenario would take the rep to the next step, which in our case was to connect the rep with another phone number for a more technical question.

"In our demonstration game, three emails were sent to each rep. One could immediately be pursued and a fifty-unit sale could be made. Another was an 'unqualified' lead, which if pursued led to nothing at all. And a third was a request for information which, over time (actually only if the rep pursued steps that took a week to complete), could be developed into a sale."

Key Learning
"The idea was to promote the learning of the corporate 'sales model' by customer service reps and sales people."

Why Mobile?
"Sales and service reps are most productive if you can train them and get them into the field quickly. When you do this you face two problems: first, the training may not really be complete when you deploy them; and second, they forget the things that they don't have to deal with every day. Our idea was to expose each rep to questions from 'simulated' customers, so they'd have to go back to the books or references, or to their colleagues, to answer the questions, and thus they could continue their learning right on the job. And what's more, the questions and the answering process would be carried out using the same tools they use on the job every day—primarily email and phone."

Making the Case
"Sales organizations didn't take to this approach. After talking with two organizations, we found that they wanted approaches that put more

conventional information in the hands of the sales force. They wanted question-answer approaches. So where did we go then? Well, we went in the direction of *fun* instead of work.

"Our process, which we developed in 2004—supports back-and-forth interactions between 'players' and a computer-based scenario—which can bring intrigue, surprise, and suspense to an interaction. The *player* doesn't quite know what's going to come next. He may not know whether an incoming email is part of a game or part of real life. So we approached the problem of how an *art museum* (or other public institution that has 'visitors') might engage its visitors in intriguing activities which would (1) get them into the galleries; (2) get them engaged in setting directions for the organization; and (3) get them into creating art; we thought it might work. And it did.

"I approached two local institutions, and Yerba Buena Center for the Arts took us up on our proposal to provide a 'thought game' to get visitors involved in thinking about what they call their 'Big Ideas.'"

The Solution

"We developed a four-step process which the player initiates by sending a text message or email to a 'secret' in-game email address. The message must include a secret word that triggers play of the game. For YBCA, the game, which we called 'Making Peace.' required sending the word PEACE to an email address.

"Because the YBCA 'Big Idea' was 'peace,' the theme of the game was to get the players thinking about peace in their lives and in the world. We worked out four steps/stages/questions for the players to answer, in sequence. As they moved through the stages of the game, they sent words, phrases, poetry, and photos that we incorporated into an online montage. This montage was also displayed within the building on a wall in the 'Room for Big Ideas' right next to the gallery entrance.

"YBCA and Red7 worked together to design the entire interaction. The only 'given' was that there would be a sequence of challenges (questions) and responses (answers), and that these would be played out using email and photos. The 'department of community engagement,' headed by Joel Barraquiel Tan, scheduled several meetings where the team discussed the questions and did 'dry runs' through the sequence of challenges.

"Before launching the game publicly, members of the YBCA community were invited to participate in order to 'seed' the game with photos so it wouldn't look like a ghost town.

"The mosaic of words, phrases, poetry, and photos is maintained online and can still be viewed (http://peace.tmpp.org/show) by the public. As with other such four-stage games, we found that some people had trouble conceptualizing even how to start the game—we fine-tuned our software to accept several misconceptions about how the initial starting message was to be sent, thus making it easier to enter the game. The iPhone first came on the scene during the run of this game, and the particular way AT&T sent text and photos had to be debugged. We ended up manually processing all photos that were submitted by game players—and we do so to this day—which also provides a built-in 'filth filter' so we can weed out inappropriate photos before they might otherwise appear on the big LCD screen on the gallery walls. Participants sent their 'best photos' and intensely personal moments to the game. Most participants dropped out after the first couple of interactions, but many played all the way through the four stages. It takes effort to think about a question, take a photo to illustrate your response, and send it by email. We were quite pleased with the participation.

"We also found that building events that served to feed more photos into the game was a really productive move for us! On 'Big Ideas Day,' which was an open-gallery day for the public, we took photos and fed those into the game and wall-mounted display. People loved it."

The Benefits

"We were able to extend the reach of the museum/gallery out into the community using this mechanism. The 'community engagement' department really got into the process and we've done several more of these games, on different themes and 'Big Ideas,' over the course of nearly two years. We have experimented with reaching different 'communities'—in our case including also the LGBT [lesbian, gay, bisexual, transgender] communities (which are quite varied, of course) in an event focused specifically on a 'state of the community' event near the end of 2009. (This game, Pink Yourself, appears at http://pink.ybca.org/.) We learn more each time we do one of these focused games."

The Results

"We saw over one hundred players over the course of a few weeks, many of whom went through all four stages of the game. In the case of Pink Yourself, there was a YBCA event one evening and the organization incorporated an in-party event whereby participants could take photos and have pin-on buttons made (as well as having the photos appear in the online mosaic)."

Lessons Learned

"Focus more on making the interaction fun or useful—not on the learning aspects. In our community games, people are thinking, learning, experimenting, but we don't point to *learning* as an outcome at all. Learning takes place informally in all of the games."

SUMMARY

I hope that these examples have helped you comprehend some of the breadth that can be seen in mobile solutions. These may serve as reference examples for you, and as you peruse the upcoming ways to think about mobile, you should look to see which were manifest here.

AN INTERVIEW WITH MOBILE LEARNING LEADER DAVID METCALF

As an independent researcher, analyst, and consultant, Dr. David Metcalf combines business sense and technology efficiencies to provide effective results. Dr. Metcalf was formerly the chief learning technologist at RWD Technologies. There he was responsible for the analysis, design, and strategic alignment of RWD's technology solutions for learning. Dr. Metcalf joined RWD with the sale of his NASA Kennedy Space Center laboratory spin-off company, Merrimac. Prior to spin-off, he was the lead multimedia designer at NASA's Kennedy Space Center. He was responsible for the management and operations of the award-winning multimedia laboratory for various government contractors. Dr. Metcalf holds a B.A. in computer graphics from the University of Texas, an M.S. in computer-based learning, and a Ph.D. in information systems from Nova Southeastern University and keeps current by continuing to hold appointments at several universities.

At the events where I saw Judy Brown, she was usually joined by David Metcalf. David has had the opportunity to lead development of a number of innovative mobile applications and continues to see coming opportunities, so I thought it natural to highlight him here when we talk about design. David was kind enough to answer some questions for us.

How did you get started in mobile learning?

We did some of our first projects using the Palm VII with a built-in radio receiver to access just-in-time information. We also saw a place for companies that wanted the one-way push of information out to the field for their mobile and remote workers.

Things got more exciting in 2003 and 2004 when the promise of two-way interaction became more of a reality with access to collaborative systems, discussion boards, chat, and more robust use of messaging. We also saw the vision that more robust technologies like barcode reading, location-based tracking, voice space, and visual search could revolutionize the user interface, making it much easier to provide a rich learning experience and just-in-time performance support.

In the past few years, we've seen compelling research that explores the learning models that can be used in mobile learning in things like mobile alternate reality games, as well as in the integration and mashup of other technologies and corresponding learning models. I've been calling this concept "learning theory mashups."

What areas are you working on that hold promise currently?

Some of the technologies and learning theories are ready for use right now. Through the use of barcode readers, standard camera phones, and visual search, you can realize the vision of point-and-shoot learning, which we've been working with for several years. Similar tools give access to voice-based search and do a very good job of capturing the spoken word from multiple speakers, even across multiple language and dialects.

Multi-modal input and output using these tools will also help deaf, hearing impaired, and blind individuals better engage in our mobile world. This also enables and supports constructivist and discovery learning techniques just in time for public support and real-time integration of learning components from distributed locations (let us say "within the cloud") that instructional designers can point to and link to without having to spend inordinate amounts of time integrating these into a single learning course or more expensive simulations. You see these techniques being used in alternate reality games, frameworks for learning, and in Google's g-learning model.

What do you foresee in the future?

There's work to do in more advanced learning theory mashups (1) to come up with the perfect, personalized learning toolkit that has the right mix of apps for a particular job role or function and (2) to use messaging in robust ways to link to learning in the cloud and come up with cohesive story-driven learning that engages learners and provides authentic assessment by measuring their real interaction in both learning and real-world performance situations.

I'm also intrigued in what the future holds in other form-factors of technology that might further enable other learning theories and performance and productivity outcomes. For instance, smart pen technology has forever changed the way that I interact with pen and paper by augmenting them with a digital interface to mobile devices, my computers, and the Internet at large for social networking and collaboration.

CHAPTER

7

MOBILE MODELS

As you have seen, mobile can serve up full courses, act as a learning adjunct, or function as performance support. We'll look at all three of these applications in this chapter, with an emphasis on supporting performance.

How do you make mobile part of your repertoire of solutions, not just make a specific mobile application? Kris Rockwell, CEO of Hybrid Learning, reiterates my own mantra: that to really "get" mobile you have to *think different.*

Easier said than done. What I can do is walk you through a suite of different ways to think about mobile. To start with, how do *you* use your mobile device to make yourself more effective? Here are some of my tricks:

■ Check my calendar for availability, and add new events to it.

■ Put in my commitments as tasks.

■ Jot down notes as things occur, and refer to notes with useful frameworks.

■ Capture or reference contact details.

■ Take pictures of events, and refer to diagrams and images I save on my device.

■ Create diagrams to capture my understanding.

- Use a browser to look up answers to questions and find information.

- Use a variety of applications to access information "in the moment" (such as checking train schedules).

- Use maps and map-linked applications to find things nearby and get directions.

- Use a variety of applications to communicate with people with Twitter, Facebook, and more.

- Play games to fill time or entertain kids.

- Store documents to be read.

Ones I do not use so much, whether due to the lack on my device, or my own personal preferences, include:

- Listen to audio files or watch videos.

- Capture audio and/or video of interviews or events.

- Augment the view through the camera with additional information depending on where I face.

And I am sure you have some I have not thought of. The goal, here, however, is to jump-start thinking. Note that *none* of the uses I've outlined above include formal courses. They are much more about performance support; in-the-moment needs. So let us start there.

When we look across these examples, a pattern emerges that gives us a way to characterize the opportunities. From these patterns we derive models that in turn are useful tools to help us think conceptually, understand the system, and then flexibly apply the concepts to different needs. In this chapter, we will review a variety of models, existing and emergent, that give us different ways to think about mobile learning. The goal is for you to find some that resonate with you initially to give you a handle on mobile learning and a reference to come back for more when you have developed those first models well.

THE FOUR C'S OF MOBILE CAPABILITY

Earlier, we talked about the seven C's of natural learning. Now we want to talk about the four C's of mobile capability: accessing *content* (Figure 7.1) in the form of media, *capture* (Figure 7.2) of information,

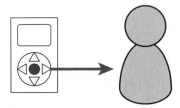

FIGURE 7.1. *Content*

the ability to *compute* (Figure 7.3) a response, and to *communicate* (Figure 7.4) people with each other. Each of these has a unique contribution.

Content

One of the common uses of mobile devices is access to media. Regardless of whether the content is dynamic, such as audio or video, or static, such as graphics, photos, and text, having information available on demand can be valuable. Frequently, this access is for convenience so that we can occupy time otherwise wasted, such as sitting during a commute, in an airport, or in line.

A more interesting opportunity is contextual access, so a video of a repair procedure can be viewed while faced with a broken device, or a job aid can be accessed while consulting with a client.

This information may be pre-loaded on the device or accessed online, but it very much is about consuming information. As a cognitive adjunct, however, augmenting our memory is a valuable contribution.

Capture

In addition to presenting information, a second possibility is capturing information. Information can be captured in a mobile device by sensors, such as a microphone or camera, and also by text entry. Other sensors can be used for data capture as well, such as via a GPS. For instance, a performance can be videotaped, notes about a situation can be taken, or contextual data can be measured.

This information can be stored until accessed later or communicated immediately to a common repository or an individual. The value of this is to share context for communication and problem solving and to capture performance for later review and reflection. A recent capability provided by Google is Google Goggles, where you can take a picture and the system searches based on image recognition.

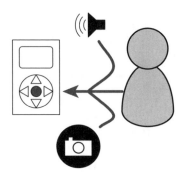

FIGURE 7.2. *Capture*

Jane Bozarth, in *Social Media for Trainers* (2010), tells of having customer service learners take pictures of the organization's premises and how a stated goal of "respect for customers" is negated in a picture of a sign stating "Prices subject to change according to customer's attitude." This is a powerful learning moment!

Jeff Tillett and Mark Chrisman from T-Mobile USA have used capture successfully several times. For one, they had customers capture videos of how they used the device successfully and received wildly creative submissions. For another, they had top performers create short videos about how they were successful, and these were highly valued by learners (and leadership!).

Compute

Many times, individuals are not good at a variety of types of computation, but digital processors can be programmed to be. As a consequence, the combination of individual plus processor is more effective. Individuals can capture data and enter it, and the device can provide processing to transform that information into more relevant data.

For instance, a client can be interviewed, and a custom configuration can be priced. Or parameters can be entered to identify a hardware fault in troubleshooting. Or incomprehensible data fluctuations can be transformed into a graph for evaluation.

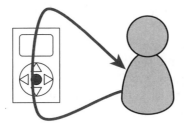

FIGURE 7.3. *Compute*

While this may require custom configuration, it is a powerful way to provide much more detailed support of individual capability. Realize that capture and computation can be combined for even more powerful opportunities, such as measuring the direction being faced and adding information about what is in a particular direction.

Communicate

One of the undervalued opportunities with mobile devices is the opportunity to connect with others, to communicate. While people regularly

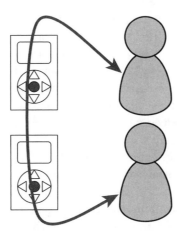

FIGURE 7.4. *Communicate*

use the phone part of a cell phone or smartphone, there are many other options available.

Communication channels supported by mobile devices include IM, microblogging, text-messaging, and VoIP in addition to the phone. Further, as seen above, mobile devices can communicate in special channels, such as serving as the basis for an audience response system.

Layers on top of these channels are also emerging as *social networking*. Applications currently exist on most smartphones for the most popular social networks: Facebook, LinkedIn, and Twitter.

FOR EXAMPLE

Microblogging

A new form of communication has emerged in recent years, embodied in the networking application (and phenomenon) Twitter. While not specifically mobile, it facilitates quick and brief exchanges in a new way.

At core, Twitter emulates text messaging in having a limit of 140 characters per *tweet* (a single twitter message). This method of communication, however, differs from text messaging in a couple of significant ways. There are some similarities with IM in that a broader reach of people can be targeted with one message and that you can specify to send to an individual person. However, there also similarities to *blogging*, in that anything not directed to an individual is available to anyone who subscribes to your tweet stream.

This form of communication has defied characterization with it's own unique properties, but similarly has delivered its own unique affordances. People have found it valuable to point to (and be pointed to) interesting things or occurrences. It's also a powerful mechanism to ask questions. An additional capability to put in *hashtags* (a set of characters preceded by a hash character) allows particular topics to be followed.

For example, I joined several colleagues, catalyzed by Marcia Conner, in launching a Thursday evening (U.S. time) chat around learning topics using the hashtag #lrnchat (with hashtags, shorter is better given the character limit). It has now expanded to a second time on Thursday mornings (U.S., evening Europe).

Given concerns over security, corporate versions of Twitter have emerged that provide similar capabilities with greater limitations on who can see messages, but retaining the social networking structure.

Social learning has been the main component of informal learning and, as the Internet Time Alliance says, "The future of e-learning is social." As we have argued elsewhere, the accelerating rate of change means that organizations will increasingly struggle to develop formal learning in time to meet needs. The answer will be, instead, to support performers to help one another, sharing lessons learned and collaborating to create new answers. Mobile devices will make this opportunity available ubiquitously and support a new level of creativity.

Combinations

You *could* think of this as the fifth C, combinations of the first four elements. *Augmented reality*, discussed later, mixes *capture* of local context by sensors with *compute* to add information onto the existing information. Similarly, using capture to share the current context with peers or experts to collaborate mixes *capture* with *communicate*.

Applying the Four C's to Different Roles and Levels of Learning

The four C's provide immediate guidance about opportunities for delivery and principles for design. If we put these categories across the top of a table, such as Table 7.1, we have the opportunity to think about how we might support categories of learners.

Consider the table and put some of your learner groups in the left-hand column, and then think: What would I connect them to that

TABLE 7.1. **Mobile Category Opportunities**

Role	Content	Capture	Compute	Communicate
Sales	product sheet	sales pitch	pricing	product expert
Marketing	sample ad	customer interview	competitive ad costs	PR company
Executive	strategy	presentation for practice	performance dashboard	other officers
Field Engineer	trouble shooting guide	aberrant performance	acceptable variation	second-level support

would help them perform? What could they capture that would be useful? And so on. Here I have filled in some sample responses, but an empty one is in Appendix C and available for download from www.designingmlearning.com.

Another way to use these categories is to think how they might be applied for both formal and informal learning, as in Table 7.2.

BEING OPPORTUNISTIC

There are stages of investment and effort that influence how you might tailor mLearning to your particular situation. These range from the obvious to the more involved.

Reactive

The first component of this approach looks at easy opportunities first. The *reactive* approach says that whatever you already have should be made available for viewing (as much as possible).

Most organizations have presentations, documents, and even audio and video clips that might of interest or use to their learners. Just as these are likely to be available on the intranet through portals, it generally is not difficult to also make them available for mobile distribution.

TABLE 7.2.   **Category by Formality**

	Formal	Informal
Content	introductions, concepts, examples	job aids, troubleshooting guides, product sheets
Capture	performance recording, sharing presentations, taking notes, diagramming ideas	capturing context, diagramming ideas, taking notes
Compute	simulations, interactive job aids	interactive job aids, custom calculators
Communicate	connect to instructor, expert	connect to expert, peer

It may also be the case that access to company directories or social networks might be easily available for mobile access, to facilitate connecting and communicating (remember, don't just think of mobile as content delivery).

And if there is an easy way for employees to upload content of their own, that is worth thinking about supporting. For example, uploading may be a core capability of your learning management, content management, or social media system.

Proactive

Proactively, a learning group could start designing their materials deliberately for mobile delivery. A redesign of the production process could yield materials that are easily viewable on any browser or easily generate both mobile and desktop versions.

Similarly, the design process might identify components from the eLearning production process that should be separately accessible as learning components (we'll discuss that in more depth later), such as charts, diagrams, tables, or examples.

This is still largely thinking about *static* content, that is, text and graphics, but audio and video that are being produced for other purposes may also qualify. Making video and audio recorders available has been a valuable way for groups to capture ideas, performance, and more.

Likewise, making a mobile version of the company directory is not a bad idea. Email, phone, IM, and twitter-like connection capabilities could be made available. In the not-too-distant future, videoconferencing via mobile devices will be not just possible, but plausible and commonplace.

Custom

The most difficult area is creating custom software for specific needs that can't be met by static content. However, even here there are levels of complexity. Several providers are offering the capability to develop once and deliver on most platforms. Without any more complicated interactions than clicking, decision trees and interactive questionnaires can be developed.

The next level, where more complex interactions and connections to dynamic databases are supported, begins to tap into real complexity. At the time of this writing, such an endeavor largely becomes a custom-programming task for each supported device. As yet, the proprietary operating systems don't support much in the way of common standards for cross-platform development.

We'll talk later about the tools for development. If you can specify it, you can build it, but it may be difficult to target more than one platform without significant extra overhead. On the other hand, those barriers are breaking down and may essentially be breached by the time you read this.

FOR EXAMPLE

Context Over Convenience

Practically speaking, much of mobile access is about convenience over bandwidth. We listen to podcasts in the car not because the audio quality might rival a home theater system (although the new headphones and digital output are very good), but because we have the time while driving. Similarly, we might watch videos during a flight, and I certainly use that time as an opportunity to catch up on reading. The point being, a lot of mobile use is serendipitous use of time rather than targeted mobile functionality.

However, I believe that one of the real opportunities at hand for mobile is very much focused on context. If we know when and where people are, we can deliver targeted information that is specifically helpful to them in that situation. This is where custom development comes into its own.

Imagine a technical company that has a client at a particular location. There would be very different information needs for a sales representative calling on that client versus what a field service representative might need. Similarly, the sales representative could need very different information when going there to renew existing licenses versus calling about a new sales proposal.

Likewise, imagine that you have learning goals associated with specific types of activities. For example, say a learning goal is to improve negotiation skills or employee coaching. If you have such an activity upcoming, preparation and/or tools could be valuable to be provided at the appropriate time. It does not matter where learners are, but very much matters what they are doing at that time.

While the capability has been in place for a number of years now, the convergence of hardware, software, and awareness mean that contextualized delivery is now a compelling opportunity for mobile delivery, and one you want to keep at the top of your mind.

The opportunity here is something you should really be excited about, however. Games (or, to be "politically correct," Immersive Learning Simulations) are the most powerful learning experience next to live mentored practice. The possibilities for learning games are a coming opportunity. Also, custom calculators and interactive decision support tools optimized for your mobile employee needs are going to be big opportunities to reduce errors, streamline sales and repair processes, and generally improve execution.

SPACED PRACTICE

Another useful consideration regarding mLearning design comes from a deeper understanding of learning. We know that one massed practice is not as effective as practice spaced over time. Will Thalheimer summarized the research in *Spacing Learning: What the Research Says* (2003), indicating the benefits of extending the learning experience.

Some parameters affect how much practice is required, the amount of time in each practice session, and the optimal time between practice sessions. These factors include the amount of time that occurs between the learning event and the performance situation, the frequency with which performance will occur, the accuracy required, and so on. Reactivating knowledge is a powerful mechanism to support retention over time.

Qualitatively, the results are that spaced practice may take longer to get to the desired level of performance, but will be much more robust in retention over time. As shown in a conceptual representation, we see less loss of ability with spaced practice, as seen in Figure 7.5.

Mobile provides a marvelous channel for just this reactivation. While practice is the most meaningful reactivation, even seeing examples can facilitate retention. And using different contexts in examples and practice in these reactivations can also be a powerful facilitator of transfer as well.

You should definitely be using scheduled follow-ups to formal learning with mobile-delivered examples and practice problems to maximize the value of investment in learning outcomes.

FRAMEWORKS

There are several ways to think about what we are delivering that come from typical implementations and frameworks. We can, and should, look at mobile learning from the perspectives of performance support, learning augment, and formal learning.

Performing

The most typical way to think "mobile" is to carry the notion of performance support forward to the mobile arena. Allison Rossett has been

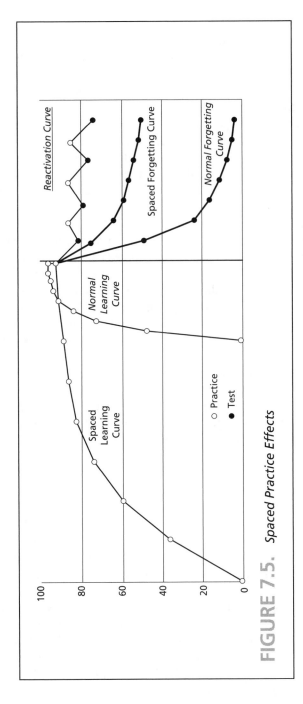

FIGURE 7.5. *Spaced Practice Effects*

Source: Adapted from W. Thalheimer. (2006). ***Spacing Learning Events Over Time: What*** the Research Says. Boston: Work-Learning Research, Inc.

a proponent of going beyond the course and thinking of performance support, and her book with Lisa Schafer, *Job Aids and Performance Support* (2007), provides good guidance about how to think about designing support. The same principles, naturally, apply to the design of mobile performance support.

The framework suggests two main categories of performance support: planners and sidekicks. They differ in when they support: *planners* come before or after the performance situation, while *sidekicks* are deployed during the performance situation. To think of it another way, we can look at how those different times can and should be supported.

Planning implies mental preparation for an upcoming event or using the outcome of an event to set up further actions. External memory can help us remember all the details that we should think about (given that we're not good at remembering details) before or after. Representations that capture details beforehand can help those aspects to be active during the activity. Afterward, we can record details that might slip away later or indicate follow-up actions. Note that plans prepared beforehand can serve as sidekicks during performance.

Sidekicks provide support during performance. Where there are gaps in our ability to solve problems completely in our heads, external resources can improve our ability to perform. Models, checklists, and other guides can support process execution. Lookup tables can supplement memory. Representation tools can capture data to facilitate comprehension.

To Course, or Not to Course

The opportunity exists to think about mLearning as a formal learning augment as well. By using an abstract model of the components of the learning process, we can also get a handle on formal mLearning. However, to be clear, the emphasis is on augmentation, not on delivering full courses.

I have argued that instructional models are not static, but are in a state of continual change. This is a positive outcome, reflecting the ongoing adaptation to accommodate new research results. In addition, I believe they're converging on a model that is an intersection of the various theories. I believe Collins and Brown's *Cognitive Apprenticeship* (1989, 1991) is where they'll end up.

FOR EXAMPLE

Cognitive Apprenticeship

The Cognitive Apprenticeship model was based on an abstraction across several innovative and insightful programs in teaching reading, writing, and mathematics with a focus on meaningful skills, not just rote knowledge.

There are several important components in Cognitive Apprenticeship, including modeling appropriate behavior, providing social practice, and initial scaffolding and gradual release of the task to the learner.

At core, Cognitive Apprenticeship is focused on skills, rather than knowledge, an approach that is increasingly relevant as the half-life of fixed knowledge drops and we have to focus more and more on meta-cognitive, or learning-to-learn, capabilities. Overall, Cognitive Apprenticeship incorporates social, constructivist, and cognitive components into one well-integrated whole.

My "elaborated" version of Cognitive Apprenticeship in Figure 7.6 includes the common elements of introduction, concept, example, practice, and summary, but it is augmented in a number of ways that reflect deep learning. This includes adding emotional engagement, contextualized introductions, and more. At core, it also focuses on meaningful skills, not rote knowledge.

I introduce Cognitive Apprenticeship as an initial way to think about augmenting learning. If we think about the core activities, we need to (as a partial list):

- Engage the learner emotionally.

- Activate relevant knowledge.

- Help the learner "get" the objectives.

- Set expectations appropriately.

- Present the concepts.

- Re-present the concepts in multiple ways.

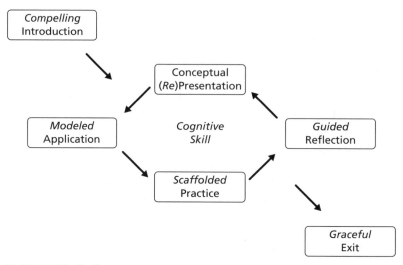

FIGURE 7.6.   *Cognitive Apprenticeship*

- Demonstrate the application of the concepts to specific contexts.

- Annotate the concept application with the associated thought processes.

- Provide meaningful practice.

- Provide sufficient practice.

- Ensure that the contexts across examples and practice span the space of application.

- Reactivate the knowledge at sufficient intervals.

- Close the experience emotionally.

- Close the experience cognitively.

- Point to further directions.

- Potentially, engage discussion around the concepts and application to meaningful problems.

These are not only good principles for learning design, but there are clear roles for mobile in all of these activities. The first way to think

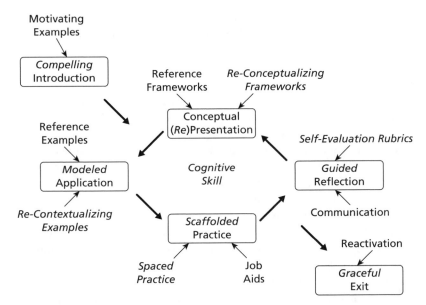

FIGURE 7.7. *Learning Components and Mobile Roles*

about it is to consider taking all the separate elements of the learning process, initial motivation, concepts, examples, practice (Figure 7.7), and so on and deliver them separately for a variety of purposes.

So we can:

- Deliver motivating examples before the learning experience.

- Present new concepts, examples, and practice to reconceptualize, recontextualize, space practice, and generally reactivate.

- Turn real performance into a learning experience by reminding beforehand, scaffolding during, and providing evaluation support afterward.

Note that any resources we provide during practice can be also provided during performance, so we can automatically create performance support. So, for example, we can take concepts as guides to performance and examples as models for solving problems. Similarly, any job aids provided during practice can also be available during performance.

All these elements are being developed in any formal learning, and automating their availability via mobile systematically provides learning enhancement.

Learnlets

There have been examples of typical asynchronous eLearning courses that have been put on a mobile device and successfully used. In one case, the audience was high-powered executives and taking a course at a desktop left them vulnerable to phone calls and in-office visits. By having the course on their BlackBerry phones, they could complete the course in otherwise useless time on planes.

In general, however, courses of any reasonable length violate the principle of having access be short and sweet. As a consequence, in general I do not suggest trying to put courses on a mobile device, but suggest augmentation as discussed above. However, there is a plausible case to be made for what some call *microcourses*, smaller courses that are just a few minutes in length.

Does it make sense that you can have microcourses that are valuable? I asked that question on my blog and received general affirmation. So then it comes down to asking what characteristics define a good microcourse.

One direction is, for me, to use minimalist approaches in creating the components. As mentioned previously, I think we under-use comics in learning and believe that we can effectively use a comic that exaggerates the negative consequences of not knowing the information (or positive consequences of knowing it) if well designed. If we accurately target context and need, this can serve as introduction by itself. Similarly, a diagram can serve as the concept, a comic strip as an example, and then limited practice.

This leads us to the second consideration, the scope of the learning objective. Ideally, the scope is something where a short presentation and chance to practice just once or so will actually help accomplish a learning objective. It is hard to characterize, but it's likely just a new way of thinking about something or a small modification, or it leverages pre-existing knowledge in a new way. It might also be about one particular feature of a product, one particular aspect of a service, or a small step of a larger product.

Increasingly, we are looking at making our content more modular for a variety of reasons that reflect our growing understanding of how learning works and takes advantage of new technologies.

Microcourses are a natural consequence of that move. As the title of my blog, *Learnlets* suggests, I once proposed that in the future, we will have lots of little interactive learning experiences that can teach us anything we need to know, including how to design little interactive learning experiences. I believe that mobile-delivered learnlets *are* microcourses, and are a valuable direction we will see more of.

SUPPORTING PERFORMERS

Two of the ways we actually perform in the world are in practiced and novel situations. Hermeneutic philosophy talks about how we act in the world when we can, and what we do when we have a "breakdown" and our practiced behaviors will not provide the guidance we need. The proposed solution is that we have to repair the breakdown, and then we can reflect and learn from the experience before we go back into action, as in Figure 7.8.

In the interest of thinking how we might use technology to support performance, I remapped this cycle from the perspective of performer needs (see Figure 7.9). If an answer exists, an individual would prefer to find it. If the answer does not already exist, support shifts to scaffolding problem solving. And if the answer *is* found, ideally it would be added to the resources available at the first step.

From this perspective, we can think about how we might want to provide resources to support performance (Figure 7.10). If we think about what information we can provide, we have a wide variety of solutions (notice that courses are only one form of solution). Learners can go back into performance if they find the answer. If we need to problem-solve, we might need data, collaborators, or process support. And when we find the solution, we need to either edit existing resources or create new ones.

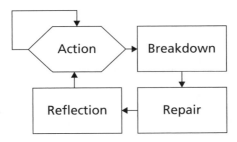

FIGURE 7.8. *Action in the World*

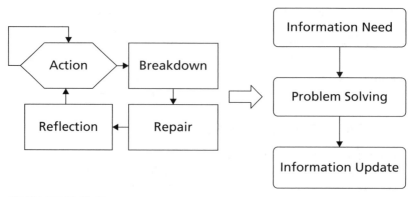

FIGURE 7.9. *Performer Needs*

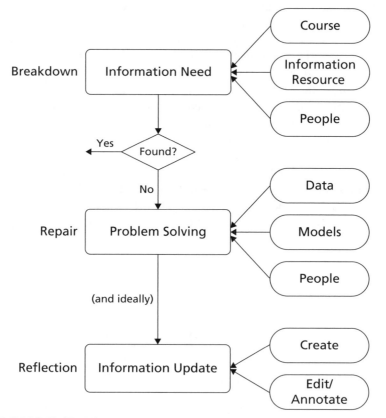

FIGURE 7.10. *Performer Support*

This is an idealized model. If we do not find the answer, sometimes we abandon the problem rather than insist upon solving it. If we *do* solve the problem, many times we immediately go back into action and do not make any extra effort to learn from the experience.

However, it does give us a much richer picture about how to support performers. This also gives us guidance about how we might use mobile devices.

DATA DELIVERY

In meeting learning needs, it can also be valuable to consider the type of data you might like to deliver. Different modalities offer different affordances, or inherent properties for communication. Each, of course, also offers tradeoffs in costs to produce and to deliver.

SMS

In much of the world, text messaging (technically simple message system or SMS) is as common as voice calls, at least in certain sub-segments of the population. One-way text messaging can be valuable to send reminders or updates. You can also make responder systems that lead the learners through a series of exchanges to present material and use their responses for linear or even branching responses. Even simple branching scenarios could be delivered. And we have seen that reactivation is a powerful learning opportunity.

In the United States, text messaging is often an extra cost, instead of being automatically included in the contract with your service provider. Consequently, automatically assuming the capability may be a mistake. On the other hand, production costs should be low.

Voice

Phones, at least (and almost everyone seems to have *some* sort of mobile phone these days), share the capability of using voice. Triggered messages can be delivered by voice, as you have no doubt experienced via auto-dialers. While care needs to be used in choosing this option, as a call may be intrusive (although being able to leave a voicemail without ringing the phone is an option), making voice a choice versus text messaging might meet some learners' preferences.

An alternative is podcasts, which similarly have production values requirements, but are made available on demand, rather than delivered to the learner.

Voice takes a bit more production capability, as audio ideally should be recorded professionally with a script and a voice talent, but otherwise the distribution is effectively as simple as text messages. This holds true for podcasts as well.

Media

One trick is to think of the media you already have available. In the content category, what do you already have in digital format that you might make available? Most organizations have a large variety of media already, but also think through the media you might create. What media might you make available?

When we are talking about pushing out media to the learner as opposed to making it available, we have to consider both the ability of the audience to handle the media and the learning value. We saw the properties of media in the foundations, and here is where we consider when it would be valuable to see a context, a concept, or both. Essentially all data has a cost, and the only issue is whether the device in question is on an unlimited data plan or whether the quantity could get costly.

What we have to consider carefully here are production and distribution. Documents are relatively easy to produce and typically lightweight in their data footprint. Audio, as above, has more production costs and a higher data footprint. Video actually breaks down into two categories: film and animation, with different production costs but similarly high data demands. Animations typically incorporate voice, graphics animation that requires graphic talent, and the overhead of coordinating the voice along with the animation. Film, when you go beyond just capturing a presentation, typically requires not only scripting, but actors, costumes, lighting, and more.

FOR EXAMPLE

Comics

One medium we ignore too often is comics. Comics strike an intriguing balance between context and concept, allowing just sufficient context to ground the action, yet by removing unnecessary details they support a useful level of abstraction. This makes them ideal for examples, whether motivating or reference. Thought bubbles are a powerful way to communicate the underlying thinking that accompanies the decisions in examples. Further, they are relatively low in bandwidth, are a popular medium in most cultures, and work well for many levels of literacy. There are successful examples, including Scott McCloud's work on behalf of Google's Chrome, and Dan Pink's book *The Adventures of Johnny Bunko: The Last Career Guide You'll Ever Need* (2008).

Interactives

Just as we indicated for custom development above, the ability to stream out interactives has upsides for both formal and informal learning and performance. Learning simulations and guided exploration environments are great learning adjuncts. The opportunity for custom calculators and dedicated decision support is also large.

Obviously, the production costs here are big. Similarly, the data requirements can be somewhat large as well. However, the opportunities are also worth thinking about, going forward.

Putting Data into Play

We can map these data approaches to roles, just as we did earlier with the "four C's," as a mechanism to consider what we might provide and how, as seen in Table 7.3.

I remember, during a mobile presentation I gave several years ago, an audience member from an engineering firm mentioned how the teams would write white papers that other teams wanted to read but didn't have time. They had someone read the white papers and recorded them for distribution as a podcast. The engineers then listened to the white papers during their commutes. They *demanded* more!

TABLE 7.3. **Media Opportunities**

Role	Sales	Marketing	Executive	Field Engineer
SMS	pricing updates	branding phrases	inspirational messages	appointment reminders
Audio/Voice	elevator pitches	radio ads	CEO messages	process reminders
Documents	product sheets	brochures	strategy white papers	troubleshooting guide
Video	customer presenta-tions	television ads	business lectures	repair procedures
Interactives	pricing guide	survey tool	performance dashboard	parts ordering

LET ME ELABORATE

Several activities are useful ways to elaborate concepts, and elaboration is a useful way to enhance the retention and transfer of knowledge. I advocate the use of social media tools such as blogs (online journals), wikis (collaborative editing), and discussion forums to meet these needs, but so, too, can mobile approaches accomplish these means. Each of the social media approaches can also be extended by adding specific contextualization where possible.

Personalization

One way to elaborate information is for learners to connect it to their own experience or intended practice. Recognizing how information explains past occurrences is one way, and another is to plan how to incorporate new knowledge in personal actions going forward. Requiring learners to capture a couple of personal reflections is valuable, and mobile tools can support such capture as well as regular desktop tools (and can happen when convenient).

Contextualization can be drawn upon as well. If learning is aligned to a particular location or particular types of encounters, personal reflections can be captured at the location. Prompting for those thoughts would be even more powerful, linking the context with the learning explicitly. The coupling of personal thoughts in a specific context is a powerful learning combination, and proactively providing reminding when in a location or event type can provide both better preparation and better performance.

An interesting opportunity would be to capture a learner's intended way to perform in the future and then remind about this when the context is appropriate!

Elaboration

Requiring learners to extend a concept is another valuable learning tool. With social media, this can be done by proposing discussion questions such as posing conflicts, contrasts, or conundrums and asking learners to respond and then comment on another's response (in a content-full way). Again, this can be done both via a mobile device and in context-specific ways.

Certainly, such discussions can be made available via mobile delivery and can be taken advantage of when convenient. If those topics are context-specific, then they can be made available when the context is appropriate. This is the approach museums take by providing a context and indicating local issues, but this possibility can be taken advantage of for organizational use as well.

Application

The most valuable elaboration is, of course, application of the concept to a situation. Any activity wherein the learner is required to make a choice, whether multiple choice or simulation or role play, can be delivered as games or quizzes via mobile. Application takes the reactivation to another level, where learners have to not just reactivate, but apply the concept to another context, broadening the base of contexts, which facilitates generalization and transfer. Ideally, the mobile applications draw on all the principles of good practice that characterize any good learning design. And this can be just a good multiple-choice question.

A more interesting situation is when real life provides a practice opportunity. If learning can be "wrapped" by providing preparation content beforehand, support during, and reflection afterward, real performance becomes a learning improvement opportunity as well. This can be done reactively, available for the learner, or proactively, triggered by context-aware systems. For example, for a new manager with a learning goal of being a better coach, a scheduled employee evaluation meeting serves as a great opportunity to prepare the managers beforehand, support them during the meeting, and ask for reflection afterward.

Altogether, we have the possibility of extending the learning by elaborating beyond a formal learning experience into the world.

DISTRIBUTED COGNITION

Another different perspective about effective levels of support comes from so-called *distributed cognition.* As captured in Ed Hutchins' *Cognition in the Wild* (1995), the concept is that we don't have (or have to have) every piece of knowledge in our heads, but our actual problem solving is accomplished in an interaction between external representations and what we know and can do. Given that our brains are not good at remembering rote details, putting information out in the world may be a more useful way to support performance than to try to have learners remember a large quantity of information.

For example, while remembering 1-800-FLOWERS might be a clever business name, you are not likely to be able to directly translate that to a number to dial. You will likely have to use the letters on the keys to decipher what numbers to press. Why? Most people don't bother remembering the letters on the dial because that information is out in the world and it's hard for our brains to remember those details *and* we do not have to.

Mobile devices these days have a phenomenal amount of storage, particularly for text (which is small digitally). Making resources available to facilitate problem solving can be a powerful form of performance support. For instance, an organization we talked to had closets full of documents in PDF format for troubleshooting and repair procedures to be used by their field service technicians on their wide variety of digital devices installed across the country. However, the technicians didn't want to take a stack of documents around with them. As a consequence, there would be two trips required to fix something: finding information about the piece that was flawed and then getting the information to repair it. A simple solution was to put *all* those

PDFs on a PDA. All those different documents would fit in a space much smaller than they took up on paper.

AUGMENTED REALITY

Another way to look at mobile learning is not from the perspective of augmenting cognition, but the reverse, augmenting reality. A number of applications recently have used new capabilities to perform interesting versions of this.

A number of years ago, a company released a simple game for Palm's Treo phone. The game took input from the camera and replayed it on the screen, but with additional information. Layered on top of the picture were (rather cute and silly) aliens coming at you that you had to shoot. As you spun around the room you were in, you'd see aliens coming from every direction, and you had to spin around, sight, and shoot them. It did not really matter where you were or where you were looking; it was randomly layered on top of the view, but it made it more real.

The principle for at least one version of augmented reality is very much the same, but much more valuable. With the combination of the camera, a GPS, and a compass, a device can know where you are and where you are looking and then layer on relevant information to that specific spot. Instead of aliens, you might see historic information, restaurants, or potential clients.

This is another take on the contextual information, but it is displaying it in a contextually relevant way. It could be audio, layered on with your location via any sort of cue (QR Codes, RFID, GPS), or video, or just data, but the extreme is to layer it right onto your regular perception like a heads-up display (HUD) does for pilots in modern fighter jets.

The design perspective is, of course, What could you layer onto the world that would be useful?

LET'S GET INFORMAL

As mentioned in the Foundations section of this book, informal learning should not be ignored. With my colleagues in the Internet Time Alliance (Jay Cross, Jane Hart, Jon Husband, Harold Jarche, and Charles Jennings), I have been looking at how organizations can and should support informal learning as well as formal learning.

Jay Cross, who's book *Informal Learning: Rediscovering the Natural Pathways That Inspire Innovation and Performance* (2005) launched the concept of going beyond formal learning into the organizational learning space, talks about how leaving informal learning to chance is leaving money on the table. So, too, with mobile learning, and of course the intersection is also an opportunity.

The fact is that, looking across the various studies, roughly 80 percent of what is learned comes from informal learning, yet we spend a disproportionate amount on formal learning. This includes searching for answers ourselves, communicating with others, creating new answers and testing them, and so on. We look for answers on our own, and we work with others to learn. This has great implications for how we should design information resources and how we should support working together.

This perspective should also affect our consideration of mobile learning. Really, the performance support focus of much mobile learning is about making the answers available to individuals who happen to be away from a desktop. Similarly, making social connections available on a mobile device meets the equivalent social need to complement the individual need.

The implications for mobile are quite straightforward: we need to make accessible the information performers may need while they're away from the desk, both task-specific information for mobile workers and information they may happen to be pondering at a convenient time. And we need to support performers looking to connect with others, share both conceptual representations and contextual data, and communicate questions, ideas, and answers. For instance, the new proximity software that lets you know who is near you by certain criteria (such as following them on Twitter) would be an example of software that could facilitate developing personal learning network opportunities.

PUSH VERSUS PULL

One dimension, at least, to consider for the solution is whether it should be push or pull, that is, whether the learner accesses it on demand (pull) or, instead, some system presents the content to the learner or performer proactively (push).

Pull is the natural modality. If our learners are aware of the available resources, understand their value, are capable of finding the capability and navigating it, just making it available is useful.

Push works when you want to develop the learners, so as to push reactivation as a learning augment or to send them contextual information when you are not sure whether they are ready to access the information on their own. A second possibility is when something has changed that they are not aware of (but usually this is an individual choosing to let them know).

Explicitly considering each is a component of looking for ways to add support.

LEAST ASSISTANCE PRINCIPLE

A colleague once told me how, with many demands for support, he tried to use the "least assistance principle" to figure out what the least he could do to help people. He was not trying to be lazy; instead he wanted to find ways to help as many people as he could!

This principle could well be considered to be the basis of John Carroll's minimalism. As captured in *The Nurnberg Funnel: Designing Minimalist Instruction for Practical Computer Skill* (1990), he trumped an instructional design manual for a complex device. He did this by not trying to teach everything, but instead by focusing on the learners' goals and providing the minimal instruction needed to help them accomplish those goals.

One of the principles I like about Carroll's work is having respect for the existing knowledge of the learners, tapping into their real-world knowledge and meaningful goals. In many ways, it is a methodology around performance support. He used cards with minimally described steps. That minimalism not only fuels performance support, but also is ideal for mobile delivery! So ask yourself: What is the least I could do that my learners would find useful?

ZEN OF PALM

In the heyday of Palm, some of the folks guiding the design of applications for that platform coined what they termed the "Zen of Palm." Fortunately, it lives on, and continues as a guide to mobile design.

One of the key points embodied was to recognize the nature of use for mobile devices. Desktop machines typically are accessed a few times a day for long periods of time, whereas mobile devices are typically accessed multiple times a day for brief periods of usage. This perspective helps guide the design of mobile support: What could a quick reference do to support the user?

Another key point was to recognize that you should not try to include all the capability of a desktop machine in a mobile platform, but should follow the Pareto rule and try to find the 20 percent of the functionality that provides 80 percent of the value.

The overall point was to focus quite clearly on ease of use, only the necessary functionality, and tune until it works seamlessly. And that's a valuable note on which to end.

 ## QUESTIONS TO ASK

1. What comes from each one of these models for your needs?

2. What other examples do you know, and do they provide any other, more general, frameworks you might want to consider?

3. How can you create your own support tools and checklists to help incorporate and leverage these frameworks in your own practice?

SECTION

BRASS TACKS

At some point, we move from good ideas about making choices about models to the actual processes of design. We need to talk about how one systematically modifies design processes to incorporate mobile learning, what the development options are (particularly in light of the rapid change in the mobile area and less convergence in tools than we see in the devices), implementation and deployment considerations, and concomitant issues.

We consider these in the following chapters:

- Chapter 8. A Platform to Stand On presents the benefits of an infrastructure approach.
- Chapter 9. Mobile Design provides coverage of Analysis and Design.
- Chapter 10. The Development It's Not About covers development issues.
- Chapter 11. Implementation and Evaluation discusses implementation and organizational issues.

CHAPTER

8

A PLATFORM TO STAND ON

Before talking about the specifics of mobile design, it is worth considering a more systemic approach to enabling mobile solutions. As an alternative to specific mobile development, another way to view mobile is as a platform that exists to support other initiatives. This is what B.J. Schone and Barbara Ludwig of Qualcomm are doing; rather than focusing on making specific mobile solutions available, they are investing first in ensuring that they have tools that support a variety of mobile needs, and then developing individual solutions on that infrastructure to support specific needs.

PRINCIPLES

This approach has several advantages. By taking an infrastructure approach, they are making mobile capability available as a resource. mLearning becomes available to support any opportunity. It is a smart investment, because the costs can be amortized across a variety of implementations. It also facilitates lessons learned being easily shared in any new implementations. Learners and performers will see a unified approach that will simplify their ability to take advantage of the mobile opportunities. And, by taking a platform approach, different elements are more easily combined as needed.

The basis of an integrated approach is to support common uses. Integrating formal and informal resources together in a way that matches how the users think about the task is key. Ideally, the tools needed are "to hand" in the workflow, where and when needed.

For one, a mobile portal capability is necessary. Too often, mobile or not, we see a vast proliferation of portals aligned with the typical organizational silos of HR, sales, and so on. Instead, the right solution is role- or task-oriented portals that are organized around the way people think about what they are doing and are designed to support multiple ways to access information (browsing by major categories as well as searching). We want this regardless of access mechanism, but mobile restrictions on screen size and mechanisms for access make the information architecture even more important. This portal approach needs to integrate different resources, be they media types (documents, audio, video), computational tools, and connections to appropriate people.

That latter component is a new and important opportunity. Providing ways to find relevant people is as true for mobile as it is on the desktop, perhaps more so. The moment of need, when it's a person, can be far more urgent in a mobile situation. Just as the social networking tools are making themselves mobile-accessible, so too should organizational social networks, communities of practice—or whatever the organization terms them.

PRAGMATICS

What this means is that you need to provide a mechanism to:

- Make information resources available: media, computational.

- Align resources with courses.

- Align resources with tasks.

- Provide meaningful practice.

- Provide a mobile portal.

- Find people.

- Upload and share what is captured.

With these resources, you can wrap mobile around formal and support informal needs.

Making it easy to create and share media resources, whether documents, media files, or other representations, is important. This supports both augmenting courses with resources and providing mobile performance support.

Once you have created the formal or informal resources, you need to make sure people can find them. Providing a mobile portal, as above, does not mean reproducing the intranet portals, which need improvement (as Andrew McAffee demonstrated, most people find the Internet, with all its variability, easier to use than their intranets). Instead, it means making a portal that's organized around mobile use. Information design for useful resources is not enough; you need an associated information architecture oriented around how people will be able to perceive and navigate to the information they need.

In addition to information resources, for formal learning you are liable to want to create assessments, at least formative ones that learners can self-check. (Schone and Ludwig of Qualcomm told me they don't even track assessments, they are trusting their learners to take advantage of resources for their own learning needs.) Done right, even multiple-choice questions can be meaningful practice; in *Engaging Learning*, I documented how scenarios are the next best practice to live mentored performance, and how even multiple choice questions can be mini-scenarios. There are already compelling games on mobile devices that raise the possibility of creating compelling "immersive learning scenarios," as the eLearning Guild's Research Report (2007) termed them, but such custom development is still problematic.

There are platforms available that connect existing LMS via mobile, existing portal solutions via mobile, and specific mobile solutions that integrate a variety of tools. There are also ways to accomplish a mobile platform using open source solutions that are built on generic web capability. The solution that will work for your organization is quite contextualized, depending on your existing tool suite, skill sets within the organization for IT support and development, the relationship between the learning unit and the IT department, the devices to be covered, your potential mobile audience, and more. And that landscape will change between the time I write this and you read it. There isn't the capability, at this time, to provide even a decision tree about considering solutions. However, it is important to understand the platform perspective and be prepared to consider the alternatives.

In addition to content and possible computed resources, connections and capture are important infrastructure components. Creating ways for learners to capture and share information, whether pictures or video, audio, or text, and graphics is a powerful infrastructure move. Similarly, making social networks, expertise directories, or other ways for performers to connect to the right contacts is a strategic move.

Overall, thinking from a platform perspective is a strategic way to make mobile possible. As Robert Gadd, president and chief strategist for OnPoint Digital, suggests, mobile will soon be seen as just part of the IT infrastructure and not noticeable on its own. However, you may find it advisable to have the experience from at least one mobile initiative beforehand. And whether it's a first initiative or built on top of an infrastructure, you will eventually need to design an individual solution.

 QUESTIONS TO ASK

1. Are you ready for a platform approach?

2. Is there a platform approach you can use?

CHAPTER

9

MOBILE DESIGN

If you don't get the design right, it doesn't
matter how you implement it.

Beyond the infrastructure perspective and talking specifically about mobile implementations, there are two issues in addressing the design process. One is what a mobile design process might be and the specific factors that you need to account for when considering a mobile solution. The second is how to make it part of your regular design process, so that mobile is a natural tool in your arsenal of solutions. One thing that is fairly certain is that, unless it fits naturally with how you do things already, mobile just will not be used.

To address the latter issue first, about how to make it part of your solution set, at least partly requires a different stance: you have to consider your area of responsibility to include not only formal learning, but also performance support and even *informal* learning. You have to be about all forms of learning, not just formal learning. This is part of a larger change in organizational roles. And it starts at the beginning, with your analysis.

FOR EXAMPLE

ADDIE

ADDIE, the acronym for the time-honored design process Analysis–Design–Development–Implementation–Evaluation, stipulates a series of steps that are necessary to design learning. It is revered and reviled, in almost equal measure, as either the right way to guarantee systematicity or a anachronistic and hide-bound impediment to creativity. And, of course, it is both, depending on how it is used.

Used properly, it provides guidance to help ensure that no elements are forgotten. Used improperly, it serves to constrain design to an approach that adheres too rigorously to principles and has no concern for the learner experience.

In fact, ADDIE can be different depending on where and how it's used. More modern interpretations include prototyping and iterative development. One thing to be clear on, though, is that ADDIE is not a pedagogical model, but instead is a process model about the steps to take and the data to collect and thus is open to different pedagogies. (And, in a side note to #lrnchat aficionados, *drink*!)

If you look at design models from other disciplines, graphic, industrial, engineering, and others, you will find models with five, four, or even three steps. I have generally used a four-step model of analysis, design, implementation, and evaluation because my audiences are not only instructional designers but also developers, media experts, or even managers, and everyone seems to be able to comprehend that model. I'll use that four-step model here.

ANALYSIS

The analysis process, in principle, talks about determining the behavioral change and the intervention. It pretty much assumes that formal learning is the likely outcome. In comparison to the ADDIE model so prevalent in instructional design, the human performance technology (HPT) model starts slightly broader, being willing to ascertain up-front whether a job aid or other performance support approach might be more appropriate than courses to meet any particular need. While ADDIE can do that, the HPT model has it more intrinsic to the approach.

Of course, the very first step is to focus on what the key needs of the organization or unit are. What changes in performance will impact the critical components of the business? If we take to heart that in an information environment our focus needs to be on a combination of tools and skills, what new tools can we provide, and what new cognitive skills will be the optimal mix that will drive efficiencies and effectiveness? And is this a situation where convenience is a powerful learner motivator or where there is a variable context for performance?

To put it another way, is this a situation where a small objective needs to be met that we can make available for mobile access in a convenient way? Is it the case that mobile is the most effective delivery device? Is there a rich skill gap and it's either contextualized to a location or where distributed practice makes sense? Is it a situation where a specific form of portable or contextualized support can really make a difference in performance? Or is it the case that a combination of skill development and a tool would really impact performance? If any of these is the case, mobile is a viable component of the learning solution.

At this point, we can and should be looking for measurements that we can impact. We should be working backward from some delta between the current and desired outcome we want to create. Note that the right impact may not be currently being measured, so we may have to create it and find a way to measure it. Our goals must be in optimizing execution against the total customer experience, or in increasing our innovation to solve problems and deliver new products and services. We could and should be looking at:

- Time to performance
- Decreased errors
- More sales
- More customer referrals
- Less time on task
- Greater customer ratings
- More problems solved per time or less time to solve
- More product or service ideas generated
- And so on

You should also be working backward from the impact you want to have to the intervention you think will have that impact. This is not unique to mobile, but now you should be considering mlearning within the repertoire of your solutions.

The next step in incorporating mobile into the solution repertoire is that the analysis of the initial problem has to be broad enough to look at all the problems that might be impacting organizational performance, and it should include a wide variety of approaches and solutions. Training is for when skills need a shift, but sometimes augmentation might be a better approach: getting the right information or processing capability might be more useful.

The associated step is to include in the audience those people who are typically out on the road, or when the audience is occasionally out and about. This includes, but is not limited to, those folks whose jobs naturally take them off-site, such as sales and service representatives. In other words, what tasks are being accomplished that happen elsewhere that can be assisted?

Finally, the last question is two-fold: What tools and capabilities can be provided or, when one *is* developing new skills, how might small activities or context-specificity make that learning stick better? What can be done to reactivate, re-conceptualize, re-contextualize, elaborate, personalize, and extend learning?

One of the big issues that comes up at this time is that any particular solution may disadvantage some part of the audience, for two possible reasons. If you are not providing devices but instead depending on the devices individuals already carry (and they are more likely to use devices they are already comfortable with), there will likely be an inequitable distribution of capabilities. Very few devices support all modes, and the devices most likely to, smartphones, represent only a fraction of all the devices out there. Consequently, you have to decide whether to shoot for a lowest common denominator, providing support to acquire more capable devices for those less inclined, or live with inequitable access. When the opportunity is convenience, inequitable access may be acceptable.

However, even if you do have a device you provide with some acceptable level of capability, it may be the case that not every individual can take advantage of it due to accessibility issues. Whether text, visual, or auditory, there may be limitations. If you are required to support full access, you may have to repurpose materials into several forms (which is not a bad idea, and is best built into the development process) or again shoot for a lower level of capability for which this approach will work.

There are, of course, additional questions you need to ask yourself in the analysis process specifically to accommodate mobile considerations. What devices are available to your audience? What are the likely data connection opportunities in the context where access will be desired? Are there any limitations to your audience? What is the performance context? What are the task issues (for instance, does the task require visual attention)? What are the context issues (for example, is it too noisy to hear audio)?

However, if you begin with a perspective of supporting performance and consider both learner skill development as well as learner augmentation, you have a good start. Will a tool do? Does the learner need skilling? or Is a combination the best solution? For either, you could and should consider mobile as a component of the solution.

DESIGN GENERALITIES

Less Is More

Here we talk about general design principles, going beyond the "Think Different" elements to a more integrated approach. Here we are looking for an elegant synergy between the Zen of Palm and minimalism, the essence of the Least Assistance Principle discussed in Chapter 7.

We are looking for a solution that maximizes the signal to noise ratio! This includes several components: our media design and our production, our interface design, and our information architecture. While I believe these principles are true for design in general, they need to be taken to the next level for mobile solutions!

Remember that our design should be aligned to the impact we want to make. What mobile augment would affect that metric? What intervention can we conceptualize and create that will deliver the delta? That is where our focus should be.

Also, this section is not intended to replicate the wealth of background in each of the associated fields, but instead to emphasize some mobile principles and serve as an initial guide that should be supplemented with depth by research or resource in the particular area.

Media for Mobile

Jakob Nielsen has written about "writing for the web," including cutting the word count, using highlighting tricks, and more. His principles are appropriate for mobile as well and cross all media. Web design principles have suggested elegance and emphasizing communication over comprehensiveness. We want to extend that for mobile delivery. (By the way, I strongly recommend Ruth Clark and Richard Mayer's *e-Learning and the Science of Instruction: Proven Guidelines for Consumer and Designers of Multimedia Learning* [2003] as a guide to the use of media for learning.)

One overarching principle is to minimize file size. While prose and even graphics can be concise, photos, audio, and in particular video can really hog bandwidth and memory space. Err on the side of brevity, and compress to the lowest resolution that will meet the constraints of device, content, and user. Err, too, on the side of graphics over deep contextualization (that is, photos and video); cartoons and animations can be compressed more easily than can images and video.

For prose, you do not always need full sentences; if phrases are sufficient to communicate, let them. Principles such as white space, highlighting, bullets, and other graphical support to draw attention help as well. It has to work for reading on what are, still, small screens. I find that I can reliably boil down prose (including my own first drafts) by at least a third, and typically half or more. I recently went back and took a sample of initial prose and final prose, and found I had taken it from fifty-eight words down to twenty-eight. You can, too.

Audio carries a similar need for conciseness. You will want to ensure that the audio is developed for listening; what works for reading is *not* the same as what works for listening, particularly if it is the only channel being used. Keeping audio use short supports both faster downloading and low storage requirements. That said, do consider using real voice talent. When the medium is low bandwidth, the difference in quality becomes important.

For graphics, consider simple diagrams. Detailed photos may lose detail even on the higher resolution screens now being seen. This may be manageable if there is a zoom mechanism, but do not assume it, verify it. In general, crop photos to keep the minimum.

The same principles hold true for animations and video. Details can get lost without a mechanism to slow down and zoom in. Try to have the images work even at coarse resolutions. And trim scripts and images to the minimum.

One of the important areas to consider is media controls. While this is important on even desktop media, on mobile it is more important.

The context may be highly variable, with interruptions both visual and auditory. Providing the ability to control the playing of media is a valuable consideration for the audience.

Information Design

Bob Horn created information mapping, and in a broader sense you want to pay attention to information design. I have personally seen a well-written job aid that failed on the basis of how it was laid out. Most concepts or guides have inherent structure, and you want to help communicate that through your representations. On mobile, you want the most cues you can provide about how things are related.

One of the principles that works for visual media is to take advantage of spatial relationships to help convey conceptual relationships. There are a wide variety of additional visual mechanisms that can help provide clues as to relationships: color, pattern, proximity, typography, shape, and connections are some of the mechanisms available.

For audio, cues can assist. Different voices, auditory signals, and announced transitions are some of the available tools. An overview of the structure beforehand can make audio more comprehensible as well.

Animations and video are powerful, particularly for causality and changes over time, and typically have both audio and visual channels to support comprehension. In addition, audience exposure to television and film means that there are well-established conventions to draw upon. However, look more to commercials than feature-length films to consider how to design for mobile delivery.

Interface Design and Information Architecture

Interface design and information architecture is a level above information design. Here we are worried about how users comprehend what their options for actions are and how to get from where they are to other related information. The interface provides the mechanism to navigate around the information or tool, and the architecture provides the structure for navigating within. Most devices will have conventions about how their interfaces work and where information is located, and it is of the most benefit to the user if those standards are used. Violations of those standards must be considered with great care to determine whether the extra overhead is worth the value of the new way of doing things.

Typically, with mobile content you are (or should be) working with smaller chunks of knowledge. To connect them requires thinking more comprehensively about how those chunks are related and then reflecting that in both the information structure and navigation scheme.

It is absolutely critical to shoot for the way the mobile performers are thinking about the task. If they consider some information to be subsidiary to other information, there should be an interface equivalent to "drill down." If a particular chunk follows another in some sort of order, there should be a "next" convention. And so on. The point is, mapping the information's inherent structure to the user in a comprehensible way that is both communicated by the interface cues and the navigation mechanism.

FOR EXAMPLE

Resolution

In the early days of the web, there were debates about what the right assumption was about screen size on the visitor's machine. The lowest common denominator was 640 by 480 pixels, but in certain environments 800 x 600 was plausible, and cutting-edge was 1024 x 768. These days, 1024 x 768 is a bare minimum for laptops, really, and we have resizeable web designs.

Mobile, interestingly, is bringing this concern back. Mobile web is big (we'll talk about this later), but the screens are small. The new 1024 x 768, I've argued, is 480 x 320, and 320 x 240 is probably the 800 x 600. (Already, new devices are finding screen resolutions beyond 480 x 320, so these concerns are going away quickly.) With a fixed device, knowing the screen resolution means you can maximize your design. On the other hand, designing in a way that separates out the content from how it is displayed gives you greater flexibility and is the way I advocate.

The Design Process

One of the phenomena affected by our cognitive architecture is our design process. It turns out that people fall into some reliable traps in design. These include:

- *Functional fixedness:* We tend to limit our use of a tool to the way we have used it in the past, even if it has other capabilities.

- *Set effects:* We tend to solve problems in the ways we have solved other problems in the past, whether or not they are still appropriate.

- *Premature evaluation:* We tend to make decisions about a proposed solution when we should merely record it and generate others before we evaluate.

- *Confirmation bias:* We tend to look for data that confirms our hypotheses instead of looking for counterfactual evidence, even though it would be more useful.

- *Sociocultural:* Many types of cultural elements can interfere, including feeling unsafe to contribute, having an inefficient team process, or a superior who will, or is seen to be willing to, take credit.

- *Expertise: E*xpertise can be a factor in several ways, such as when insufficient expertise is represented on the team or someone's expertise can give him an undue voice.

As a consequence, I created a set of rubrics to follow to help avoid these traps. These rubrics are worth repeating here:

- *Team Design:* The cliché that "the room is smarter than the smartest person in the room" holds true, with a caveat: *if you manage the process right.* In this case, err on the side of diversity in the team. I am continually delighted by inspiration that comes from listening to those from other disciplines and back-grounds.

- *Egoless Design:* A companion to a diverse team design is ensuring that everyone feels free to share and everyone respects the others' contributions. That does not mean avoiding criticism, but keeping it focused on the positive outcome, not negative on the person or even the idea.

■ *No Limits Analysis:* When the analysis is done, but before looking at what others have done, I like to consider what we might do if we had magic. Arthur C. Clarke famously said "Any truly advanced technology is indistinguishable from magic," and I maintain that we essentially do have magic now, in that we can pretty much put any information to any person at any time in any form if we wanted to. The limits are no longer the technology, but instead the limits are between our ears (and in our pocketbooks). Thinking about what would be ideal is a great way to focus on core principles, and it is surprising how far we really can go in coming close to magic.

■ *Kitchen Sink Analysis:* A companion to thinking without limits is to be exhaustive. You should really consider what others have done, what others tried and failed at, what's close in terms of similar problems or solutions, and so on. Many years ago, a couple of interface design authors suggested that we should plagiarize as far as our lawyers will let us. The point is not to reinvent the wheel, but instead to look at everything *and* the kitchen sink.

■ *Systematic Creativity:* This is not an oxymoron; we know what certain processes yield better outcomes than others. For example, after being presented with the results of the analysis, design team members should consider their solutions independently, before coming together and sharing. All ideas should be put up without evaluation, and methods used to expand the potential solution space. Wild and crazy ideas should be encouraged. Evaluation should not begin before the potential solution and inspiration space is exhausted.

■ *Three Strategies Design:* From user interface design, we learn that when it comes to designing for humans, a waterfall (linear from stage to stage) model will not work. People are far more variable than concrete or steel. We need a design process that provides us with support for testing and refining. Hence, the guidelines are to follow *situated* (aware of the context of use), *formative* (doing evaluations to inform the design), and *iterative* (testing again and again and again).

■ *Double Double P's:* When developing iteratively, you need representations to test. I strongly recommend using the least expensive technologies available. If you invest too much, it is easy not to want to throw away what you have done, yet *revolutionary* prototyping, throwing away, is strongly encouraged over *evolutionary prototyping*, where you keep building on top of what you have already built, particularly in the early stages. I had a colleague who insisted that no coding be done until the design was fully storyboarded, which led to my P's: *postpone programming, prefer paper.* Frankly, paper is a powerful prototyping tool that is underused. 3-by-5 cards and Post-its are great prototyping tools, particularly for mobile learning.

And, yes, this is an ideal, and your ability to execute against these principles will be limited, but better to try to approach them as best you can than forget to consider them!

DESIGN SPECIFICS

There Are No Right Answers, Only Tradeoffs

Once you have identified the parameters around the need and are considering mobile as at least part of the solution, you need to start thinking about how to design and deliver the solution. There are many considerations and tradeoffs to be considered.

We really are talking about three different situations here:

- The learnlet

- A formal learning augment

- A performance support augment

Let's take them in order.

The Learnlet

The goal here is not to reiterate how to design a course, or it should not be, but to consider what we need to do differently when designing a course for mobile delivery. When we think of a full learning experience, we think of an objective, aligning the performance to the objective, and then lining up the introduction, concept, example, and practice to achieve that performance. There is no difference here, except, as we discussed above, in the scope of the objective and the associated content. How do we boil it down?

Let me be clear: our existing courses are bloated. And the principles that work for mobile delivery should also be seen in practice in non-mobile courses. As a consequence, let me list the principles, for the record.

Your analysis should not have indicated that a course was the right solution unless there was either a small enough objective for convenience of access to be plausible, or an absolutely compelling reason that a mobile-accessible course is desirable. For the latter, it might be that the employees will never be able to complete it at any other time due to distractions. Objectives should be developed in terms of several criteria:

- Focused on achieving a meaningful change

- Equip the learner to be able to do something new, not just to know something new

- Contextualize in terms of when and where this performance is expected

- Measurable in terms of defining how you know when the ability has been acquired

FOR EXAMPLE

WIIFM

WIIFM stands for *What's in It for Me*. It's about recognizing, and respecting, that learners have goals that they care about, and that you should be aligning the material you present to them to be very focused on what matters to your learners.

It is pretty simple, really. Learners are more open to learning when they understand why it is important in the larger picture—and they care about that task. In designing engaging practice, I talk about two forms of meaningfulness: (1) a problem that the learners understand is real and (2) setting it in a context they recognize and care about.

This alignment of meaning needs to permeate your learning design: from the objectives you use to design that should make a real contribution to the organization, through the objectives presented to the learners that should be clearly relevant, to the contexts seen in examples and practice that the learners should recognize as important and interesting.

So how do we consider minimizing a course for mobile delivery?

In general, I talk of objectives presented to the learner, but in a learnlet I might consider an initial motivational example that is an abbreviated combination of the emotional "hook" that helps the learner viscerally comprehend the need, the awakening of relevant knowledge, and the outcome or objectives. Such an example could humorously or dramatically exaggerate the specific and negative consequences of *not* having the knowledge or the positive consequences of having the knowledge. (I tend to prefer the former, humorously, as a default, but that's just me and really it highly depends on the audience.) So, for example, a learnlet on hooking the learner in emotionally might have a cartoon of a learner inside a (clear) box labeled "I don't know why this is important to me," and consequently unavailable to the instructor.

Done as a quick story in any medium (audio or text narration, comic strip, animation, or video dramatization), a motivating example would combine the elements of cognitive activation and emotional resonance to set up the concept presentation. Note that such an example is being used to emphasize the importance of the knowledge, not the mechanism. So it should show the situation and the consequences, but not illustrate the concept. A motivating example is to prepare the learners, not instruct them.

An alternative approach would be to show a problem that the learner understands is important, before presenting the relevant concept. This problem-based or case-based approach has proven useful in other settings, and returning to show the solution serves as an example as well.

The next step, of course, is to present the concept. While many methods are possible, I think we under-use diagrams as way to represent conceptual relationships as spatial relationships. With proper labeling, such a diagram can convey much of what's needed, concisely. Carrying on from the previous example, I might have a diagram indicating success in learning coming from both cognitive and emotional readiness.

By integrating the concept into a reference example (different from the motivating example above), we can map the concept directly to the situation, illustrating how the concept guides performance in the context. Here, we might show a video with a designer documenting both how a cognitive and emotional hook to a course was added, and the result.

If a quick practice follows that requires the learner to similarly apply the concept, we've created a small course. So a learner might be choosing among three micro-course openings and having to discriminate which addressed both issues.

Using a minimalist approach means that this could potentially be presented as five quick screens: intro, concept, example, practice with feedback, and a summary.

There have been situations when a full course has worked on a mobile device. The situation was when a compliance course was needed, but was not being taken by the higher-level staff that needed to complete it. When it was made available on a BlackBerry, completion rates went up. The hypothesis was that, in the office, these folks were in demand and could not sit at their desks without being interrupted personally or by phone. On planes, however, with no ability to communicate, they were able to complete the course. Overall, I would not expect the outcome to be impactful on the audience's learning behavior, but I do know that completion and post-test results went up.

Still, in general, I would not put courses on a mobile device, and instead would focus on augmentation.

A Formal Learning Augment

For formal learning, there is a viable argument for augmentation of a formal course. The question then becomes how to systematically design augmentation into your formal learning course. The answer lies in when and how to stretch the learning experience. There are two main approaches.

The first answer is to reactivate knowledge. This can take several forms. We can:

- *Re-conceptualize*—Using different representations to communicate the concept facilitates comprehension and application in several useful ways. And Spiro's Cognitive Flexibility Theory tells us: it gives us new ways to initially comprehend the concept, it gives us more patterns to activate the concept in performance situations, and it gives us more models to apply to solve the problem. This is very useful when the concept is complex. Presenting different ways to think about the concept, different models, is valuable here.

- *Re-contextualize*—Providing the concept applied to more contexts facilitates abstracting the concept and defining the breadth of application. By seeing what remains constant and what varies, we can discern what is inherent in the structure versus what is tied to the context. In short, we are facilitating transfer. This really helps when the concept has a broad area of application. Looking for more situations in which the knowledge would be useful (or where discrimination is critical, where it is not applicable) would be valuable.

■ *Re-apply*—Providing more practice both helps extend the re-contextualization and provides more application experience, which facilitates transfer and, of course, fine-tunes the skills. Practice makes perfect, so more practice (spaced over time) is really helpful when performing correctly is critical. Here is where capturing the breadth of situations that characterize variations in how this knowledge is applied would be useful.

A more specific and valuable form of learning augment is to go beyond just reactivation and to provide context-specific learning opportunities. If learning is specific to a particular location (for instance, Factory A), or categories thereof (say, all of the retail outlets), those spaces can be instrumented so that the device is aware of the relevance and can be triggered to provide particular information.

We can also look for categories of types of events and see when they are occurring and support them. If there is a particular learning goal that is tied to a type of event (such as a coaching meeting or a negotiation), we could recognize those types of events and deliver specific learning information.

We cross a thin line in the latter case, where we might also want to take a performance support perspective.

A Performance Support Augment

Designing a performance augment has to start with the cognitive skill that is being executed and how it needs support. What capability can we deliver that will complement our cognitive capability? The purpose here is not to suggest how to design performance support, as Allison Rossett and Lisa Schafer's *Job Aids and Performance Support: Moving From Knowledge in the Classroom to Knowledge Everywhere* (2007) does an admirable job of that. The real issue is to consider when we would want to deliver such support via mobile, and what we need to do differently for mobile.

When you want to use mobile is driven by several questions:

- *Is the task in a fixed place, or does it vary in location and time?* If individuals have to be performing in more than one context, you already have the need for something portable.

- *Will they have a mobile device already?* If they do, it's easy to put it on the mobile device rather than provide an extra thing for them to remember.

- *Is the quantity large?* If the amount of information to be provided, such as a product catalog, troubleshooting for a large variety of devices, or some other large quantity of information would be useful, digital storage is liable to be preferable.

- *Would media beyond prose and images be useful?* If so, a mobile device is likely to be the most feasible mechanism.

- *Is interactivity needed?* If the nature of the necessary support means that it is computational in nature, whether processing data or user interaction, then a mobile device is a necessity.

- *Is capturing data necessary?* Do they need to capture audio or visuals? These days, digital devices are the viable approach to manage this.

- *Is* communication *necessary?* If they need to reach someone, a mobile device is pretty much the only answer.

The answer to these questions helps determine whether a mobile performance support solution is desirable. Then we come to the issue of how to design it once we've decided we need or want a mobile solution.

What's the Least I Can Do for You?

The "least assistance principle" is your best guide here, recognizing that, despite advances in mobile device capabilities, we are still working with limited bandwidth. As a consequence, figuring out the minimum that will help is probably the maximally effective solution.

This can still be a quite in-depth guide, as we did creating a multi-level, multi-step support tool for negotiation in a previous project (documented in Metcalf's *mLearning* book, 2006). The SMEs model of negotiation has four major stages and, for each stage, four component steps. For each step, there were several questions you should be asking yourself. We took that content, and put boiled down versions of the questions for each step on one screen. Our information archi-tecture was a metaphor of horizontal navigation between the stages, and vertical between the steps. The goal was not to make a monolithic tome, but to provide the most useful support in the minimal way for each and every step of each stage.

The principles you would use to design a job aid apply here also. How do we represent this to make a minimally intrusive, maximally usable tool? We want to strike that perfect balance of just enough functionality without overloading capability. We get this by exploring both sides of the equation, and by testing.

Use the Right Medium for the Message

Reviewing the properties of media, we come to some realizations about which does what well. Each has unique characteristics, though there can be overlap.

SMS is a "push" technology that puts information out to learners and it is ready for them when they notice or check their messages. Microblogs are similar, but require the learners to be "following" the source (although that can be enforced). Email is similar, but not all devices have that capability. On the other hand, email can carry con-siderably more content and have attached media.

Text, in general, is great for conceptual information. Diagrams can do the same, capturing the relationships and using coding to convey additional dimensions.

Media such as audio and video require time to communicate. They inherently occupy at least some brain-processing capacity while their message is being presented. On the other hand, audio doesn't require attention in a specific direction, so if you need to get attention regard-less of where the learner is focusing, or if the user needs guidance while visual attention is directed elsewhere, an audio file is valuable. Images and video can convey valuable context, supporting contextual performance. This is worth considering both for content presentation and capture as well.

The issue is deciding what sort of support is most useful, what medium will convey that information most appropriately, given the devices available.

Context Is King

The other issue is what the context of learning and performance is and whether context-specific information is valuable. What would and should you do differently for one person in this location versus another person in the same location, and likewise, what would you do differently for this person in one location versus the same person in another location?

One possibility is that the context can be the source of information. For instance, a device could contain an RFID or Bluetooth transmitter that conveys the information or a QR code that points to a useful URL where content can be found.

Or the device itself could use information such as GPS location to determine where you are and what you are doing. Or the system could look at your calendar and determine what you are doing, and consequently provide appropriate information.

Just having the capabilities may not be enough, but having a proactive system may be time-saving or uniquely valuable.

Overall, performance-oriented design is a careful match of capability to need, while working under the constraints of mobile device capabilities.

GET YOUR HANDS DIRTY

The real trick, however, is to decide to take on a mobile initiative. Typically, this is not a full course (or even a learnlet), but a small tool augment. It may be easier to do a learning augment than a performance support augment if you are in a learning group, but in either case it should be small in scope, easy in implementation, and ideally large in impact.

At T-Mobile USA, Jeff Tillett and Mark Chrisman got traction with the training department by taking a very small step at first, just adding a downloadable mobile support tool at the end of the class. This did not intrude, so it was easy to get approval, yet provided learner approval, and consequently the sponsor came back with ideas for how to extend another course.

I argue that most organizations should try an eLearning initiative to gain the experience before they start trying an eLearning strategy. I feel the same for mobile learning. Try something, *anything*, just to have that experience and perspective under your belt. Even if it doesn't come about, the thinking through of design and delivery are important issues. Which, naturally, brings us to the next topic, development.

QUESTIONS TO ASK

1. Has your analysis led to a hypothesis of a real business impact for mobile?

2. Have you considered all the relevant factors?

3. Have you explored broadly enough the possible solution space before converging?

CHAPTER

10

THE DEVELOPMENT IT'S NOT ABOUT

If you get the design right, there are lots of ways to implement it.

After we have designed what we want the solution to be, then we need to evaluate the options we have for delivery. Before we can go into the details of development options, however, there are some characteristics of the mobile playing field we have to cover.

THE GOOD, THE BAD, AND THE UGLY

The environment for delivering this capability is dependent on not only the devices, but the OS and the networking providers. This creates some . . . issues.

The Good

The good news is that there are some standards that are broadly in use, and some that we can use to our specific advantage. This includes media file formats and content delivery formats. For media formats, there are fairly ubiquitous standards for video and audio that will work across a wide variety of devices. Moreover, there are converters (even free) that will switch between these formats reliably. So Microsoft's Windows audio file format (WAV, from Waveform Audio) can be converted to the standard MP3 format. Similarly, MP4 files for video can be converted to Windows video format (WMV for Windows Media Video) and back.

The formats for the web are similarly ubiquitous. While there used to be special mobile web formats (wireless application protocol or WAP) that were coupled with specific writing format (wireless markup language or WML), now most mobile browser can read plain HTML and deal reasonably elegantly with large web pages. Moreover, you can now detect the browser size and have different web pages served up at different sizes.

More powerful web formats, such as XHTML and XML with CSS, can separate content from how it looks and, with good design, provide pages that resize smoothly. Browsers on mobile devices now can read those files appropriately. There are sites that will check the quality of your web pages for conformance with standards to facilitate the use by a variety of browsers, and the W3C (the organization that governs web standards) is working on mobile standards as well.

Other common formats deliver such resizable information. Kris Rockwell is using a powerful and well-supported open source standard for information called DITA (for Darwin Information Typing Architecture), developing simple delivery software on platforms that are not already capable of reading DITA output, and making navigable content that you write once and run on any device.

Naturally, tool providers are working hard to also meet the growing need for supporting information delivery across devices. Companies like OutStart and OnPoint have systems that let you author at a high level and handle the delivery to devices.

The Bad

On the other hand, some standards are not yet well established. The major problem is moving beyond content to interactivity. As of yet, no winner has emerged to enable designers and developers to focus on capability instead of on implementation.

Flash, Adobe's animation and programming environment, which is the *lingua franca* of interactivity on the web at the time of writing, is currently problematic on mobile devices. Some will not support it, or cannot, as it can be processor-intensive and one of the tradeoffs to make processors small is to lose some of their raw speed to maximize battery life.

The only alternative, for now, is to develop in Java, which is a full programming language with all the power, and complexity, that entails or in the special software development kits specific to platforms. If you want to go beyond navigable content or web-based processing, you are going to have to limit your target devices, unless you have a *really* large budget.

As processor capabilities improve, more devices will run Flash, if Adobe can focus on efficiency instead of adding features until the devices catch up. Another alternative is a new web standard, HTML 5, which is being developed to provide interactivity as well. However, the standard is not yet finalized, and standards-body work can take a long time, as well as market implementation following standardization.

The Ugly

While device capabilities are converging and standards are emerging, there are barriers preventing the real convergence that would really benefit the mobile market, particularly in the U.S. The carriers want to put up as many barriers as possible to making it easy for consumers to switch. Consequently, they try to limit what can be done across platforms.

The lack of interoperability between providers has been exacerbated by the hardware manufacturers providing their own operating systems. Each platform runs a proprietary OS that limits the flexibility of how easily what you develop can run across multiple devices. From Palm's original OS, BlackBerry OS, Nokia's Symbian system, Windows Mobile, Apple's OS, Palm's new Web OS, and Google's Android, there is limited ability to develop once and run anywhere. Solutions are emerging, and simple media are already easy, but there will continue to be cross-platform challenges in more complex development for a while.

Even if you are not using mobile phones, you may still run into issues such as the ability to use Apple's media delivery capability (iTunes, in particular). As this point, the best recommendation is to use standards and open approaches when you can and, when you need more, to consider carefully the alternatives and tradeoffs.

DELIVERING CAPABILITY

So what do I mean when I recommend "Use standards and open approaches when you can"? We will get to the "when you need more" soon.

When we think through the 4 C's of mobile (Content, Compute, Capture, Communicate) presented in Chapter 7, we are really talking here about the first two. Capture is more dependent on the capabilities of the device (if it has the ability, it likely has the software), and Communicate similarly. So how do develop content for availability? and How do we develop interactive capability?

The first solution is either putting what you have up for access via a portal or converting it first to standard formats.

Standard Formats

The nice thing, in general, is that there are some fairly common formats available for many types of content. Email is a standard that was established well before mobile delivery became an issue. The text-messaging standard is used around the world, and MMS is similarly pretty much ubiquitous. And MP3 and MP4 (also known as MPEG-4) are ubiquitous standards for audio and video, respectively.

Now many businesses use Microsoft's Windows as the operating system, and Microsoft has developed it's own audio and video formats, .wav (audio for Windows) and .wmv (video for Windows), respectively. Unless you have chosen a Windows mobile operating system (which was renamed from Windows Mobile to Windows Phone while this was being written) device, however, you are unlikely to be able to watch those on any given mobile device. Fortunately, converters are easily available, even free, that will convert formats.

New formats for video include H.263 and it's successor, H.264. These are becoming fairly widely supported. H.263, in particular, has been supported by Adobe's Flash product, although Flash is not widespread on mobile devices despite Adobe's efforts (see above).

For documents that combine graphics and text, a format that is widespread on desktops is the portable document format (PDF). This format provides many advantages, and consequently most mobile devices of fairly general capabilities (read: smartphones and PDAs) can display PDFs. However, another standard also offers some useful opportunities.

Mobile Web

As mentioned in the discussion of resolution earlier, devices are getting larger screen sizes. Consequently, for any device that has a browser, however, going forward, mobile web is now a delivery option. And, as we noted earlier, that is no longer just smartphones, but pretty much all cell phones, tablets, and even handheld gaming platforms. Which means mobile web is a fairly viable delivery option.

There are some requirements about making content available for mobile web, naturally. Formatting for small windows, making pages resizable, having consistency in layout, providing a point-and-click interface (avoiding text input), conciseness, and using low-bandwidth media are major keys to mobile web delivery.

Content Tools

Another alternative is to use tools specifically developed for delivering mobile content. As mentioned above, Kris Rockwell of Hybrid Learning is using DITA and writing readers for any platform that does not have a browser (much more flexible than custom programming every solution).

Similarly, both of OutStart's and OnPoint's tools allow content development at a high level and have readers for most platforms. There are several other tool vendors as well. As a consequence, teams or individuals can easily develop content of varying depth (meaning that the content is rich enough to navigate through to what you need) and deliver across most mobile device platforms.

FOR EXAMPLE

Content Models

One of the areas I have been active in and am a strong advocate of is *content models.* What I mean here is having a structure you develop content into. I wrote many years ago about why you should carve up content into chunks at the level of their instructional role, for instance, separating examples from concepts and so on. As I indicated earlier in carving up Cognitive Apprenticeship, having the smaller units makes delivering learning augmentation easier.

There are significant reasons to undertake a systematic effort at integrating content development across the organization. There are cost savings in reducing redundant development as well as flexibility in delivery. There is also overhead in the initial content management systems and in the integration of efforts across within-organization boundaries.

To convey a fairly common occurrence, marketing creates product specifications, and operations fleshes the specifications out into requirements that are then developed. After the product or service is developed, those materials are passed on to three separate groups: sales training for the sales team, customer support training for the level 1 and level 2 support, and to the documentation teams for manuals. Each of these groups rewrites the materials. As an alternative, consider that marketing writes into a template that operations elaborates on and that the three groups then merely elaborate on rather than rewrite.

This is not necessarily easy, particularly crossing traditional business unit separations, but the efforts can have a big payoff. On a project that I was working on, we took what was written for the print manual and auto-populated the online help system as well (that used to be written by software engineers; generally a bad idea). We would have been able to support the customer training as well, but that group opted out (and later were surprised to find out that since we had not engineered in that capability initially, it would not be easy to remedy).

For mobile learning, effort up-front to think about the content development process from a perspective of flexible delivery (for example, so that print and web are automatically generated from the content base) means that with minimal effort, mobile content can be generated as well. The separation of the content from how it is formatted means we can write a separate mobile format and deliver the same content. The work up-front requires documenting the inputs and all desirable outputs, but that initial work is amortized across subsequent content development, reducing redundancy in development, and increasing flexibility in delivery. It also is a first step toward adaptive delivery.

As devices proliferate and content becomes more capable (print delivery being able to incorporate animation and even interactivity in the new digital eReaders, for instance), device independence will be a significant advantage. Do consider the benefits to thinking about content development from a flexible delivery perspective and equip yourself for new devices that will be coming.

Custom Programming

The barrier hits when you actually want to go to a *compute* solution. When you want to provide the performer with access to a live data stream or perform some proprietary or complicated input processing, you are likely to have to go to a custom-programmed solution. This used to be a difficult challenge, as the programming environments were embryonic and the available memory on the devices was very limited. The only benefit was that screens were so small they limited what you would want to do!

The mobile environment has changed in several ways, however. While some platforms (such as handheld gaming platforms) are still limited, the smartphone platforms (Android, WebOS, iPhone OS, Windows Mobile, BlackBerry OS, and Symbian OS) all are offering fairly rich software development kits (SDKs) that make programming a reasonably high-level affair (meaning you do not have to get down to machine-level coding).

As a consequence, while you will need programmers (this, in general, is not a task for an instructional designer), development time is not astronomic and can be fairly predictable.

Cross-platform development, however, is largely not an option. While Java Mobile Edition (Java ME) and Qualcomm's Binary Runtime Environment for Wireless (BREW) do provide some cross-platform development capabilities, there are limitations and entailments. In general, for cell phones these two environments will work but may not work on all smartphones and on other devices, for a variety of reasons.

Note that, by the time you read this, there likely will be cross-platform tools that let you develop high-level interactions and pull in a variety of sources and can deliver to a variety of platforms. There will always be new platforms that lag in having that capability, but the take-home message should always be: If you can design a useful solution, you can get it developed.

 ## QUESTIONS TO ASK

1. Are you automatically converting what you can?

2. Are you developing processes that will auto-populate mobile in the future?

3. Have you ascertained your ability to custom-develop for mobile?

CHAPTER

IMPLEMENTATION AND EVALUATION

If you build it, they may not come. There are several components to successfully testing, deploying, and capitalizing on mobile solutions. These components include managing and governing the implementation, managing the change, and evaluating the outcomes.

IMPLEMENTATION PLANNING

Implementation is not just a matter of deploying. You need a plan that includes timelines, roles and responsibilities, and checkpoints. You want to manage the rollout as a success, and to do so you need to ensure that your promises and outcomes are in synch.

One of the key components is a limited-basis trial whereby some representative set of the population actually puts the solution through its paces. It may be as simple as ensuring that the solution can be downloaded and viewed on all appropriate devices, or as broad as having a stress test where a number of representative individuals go to extreme measures: uploading large volumes of large videos, computing on extreme data cases, or a number of folks trying to use communication tools simultaneously.

You must build testing and revision into your timeline. You may not need it, but it is far better to have the time and not need it than the alternative.

You also have to manage the external impact of the project.

ORGANIZATIONAL CHANGE

As Jay Cross and Lance Dublin point out in *Implementing eLearning* (2002), successful learning technology implementations need to be handled via change management processes. The guidance they provide about managing this aspect is critical. The introduction and use of mobile learning is an organizational change that will have the same requirements as other organizational changes. These changes include messaging, support, and incentives.

Successful organizational change starts with support and buy-in from above. Whether it is a stealth operation as a first initiative or an organization-wide deployment, those affected need to approve. This includes, at least, both the immediate learning unit management and the management directly above whoever the target audience is. It may also require buy-in and support from the IT unit if their infrastructure is involved. Larger initiatives will need larger buy-in.

Their support is more than budgetary and permission. Initiatives are more successful to the extent that the representative leaders participate, actually using the solution if appropriate, but at least speaking publicly in support and discussing the behaviors and benefits they expect to see. Ideally, they also indicate the concrete rewards for participation, either directly as incentives or the increases in performance that will lead to better outcomes.

With an implementation plan and this support, active messaging can begin. Focus on the benefits to the individual rather than the benefits to the organization, although the former can certainly be contextualized in the latter. Ensure that promises are kept about timelines and outcomes.

Consider what the barriers are to individuals acting in accordance with your desires:

- Are the incentives in place actually going to suggest different behaviors?
- Will old habits kick in and lead to back-sliding?
- Are there new skills that need training beforehand?

There are many ways for a project to go awry: anticipate and prevent them!

MANAGEMENT AND GOVERNANCE

Once the program is in place, it will require ongoing management, and most projects also require governance. Just as an organization has both management to run it and a board to oversee strategic directions, so too do initiatives need management and oversight.

Management is the policies and procedures that guide operation, and *governance* is the strategic oversight to look at the operation in the broader context. There are relationships between the two, for instance, good managers are consciously working in the strategic context, but neither should be taken for granted.

Management requires responsibility for success, procedures for execution, and policies for handling problems. Ongoing monitoring of content development, hosting, and evaluation is desirable. If users can *capture* content, who is responsible for checking accuracy, determining when it should be removed, and so on? How is the directory to *communicate* with folks developed and maintained? These are not difficult issues, but they should have clear roles and policies attached.

For example, one of the common problems seen in information repositories is legacy content that is no longer valid. It has to be someone's job to ascertain when content or capability requires updating or termination. Establish responsibilities, perhaps even a matrix structure with content role by domain or topic.

A related topic is the issue of *intellectual property:* Who *owns* the content generated and the associated copyright? While this comes into play initially for employees charged with generating content (such as instructional designers and technical writers), when users start generating content, the policies should be established and made explicit. This will be more important when you start including customers and other stakeholders in the dialog who are not employees. You may have to establish policies that require agreement before using the capabilities provided.

Governance involves representatives from the stakeholders who oversee the overall approach, determine whether the components are working well, and decide how the operation can be improved, expanded, reduced, or ended. For an initial or informal project, that might just be a series of conversations with affected stakeholders. As mlearning grows within the organization, however, it will likely be advisable to eventually form an official governance board and schedule regular strategic reviews.

EVALUATION

Management typically requires evaluation. If you are developing mobile solutions, how do you know what is happening with them? Without data, how do you know whether your mobile initiative is going well, needs tweaking, or should be put out of everyone's misery?

Data can be of many types, and different initiatives can have different evaluation schemes, but you really should be looking to see what the outcomes are. As Ellen Wagner, at the time Adobe's elearning evangelist, said in a mobile panel: "If you are not measuring, why bother?"

FOR EXAMPLE

Issue: Tracking and Reporting

Many, particularly learning groups, are likely to want to track the usage of any mobile-developed solutions. In particular, for any learning content, the outcomes of any assessments would ideally be reported back to an LMS. There are several different lines of thought on this.

Barbara Ludwig and B.J. Schone of Qualcomm told me that they have focused on capabilities to get information out to performers and have not worried about LMS integration. Their attitude is: Make it available, and if learners find it of value, they can use it. The implication is clear: make sure what you develop is of value to the learners or performers. Using an iterative design process with participation and formative evaluation by individuals is a critical component.

On the other hand, learning units, particularly if compliance or incentives are involved, will want to track learner performance. Many tools now can integrate with LMSs through various application programming interfaces (APIs), and likewise some LMS vendors have added mobile delivery and reporting to their systems. This trend will only continue as mobile devices become the interface of choice in all situations not at the desktop, and those situations are on the increase.

Regardless, in most cases it should be possible to determine whether a solution was accessed, even if there is no record of use. Our ability to track usage is only going to become more robust, as well.

Qualitative data, such as user reports, is one form of valid data. Representative samples of the audience can be surveyed for feedback. Quantitative data, such as percentages of the potential population using mobile solutions, is another form of data. Downloads from or uploads to a portal can often be measured. Similarly, any mobile web applications should be able to be tracked.

When it comes to evaluating the impact of a learning initiative, I strongly believe that Donald Kirkpatrick's four levels of evaluation (*Evaluating Training Programs,* 1994) make sense, *if used properly.* That is, figure out what the organizational change needs to be (for example, "If we could just impact X, we could save/earn the organization $Y million a year," where X could be better decisions). That, ultimately, is the goal you want to achieve, and is your level 4 objective. Then you work back through observable behaviors (level 3, seeing whether the performer is persistently demonstrating the changed behavior), and an assessment of learner performance after the learning intervention (level 2, via a summative assessment), to a subjective evaluation of the learning experience by the learner (level 1, mostly useful for improving the learner "experience"). (I like one extra level I heard a client mention, level 0: essentially "Are they even 'showing up' for the learning experience?") Level 2 is not necessarily useful when you move to a performance support use instead of a formal learning experience.

If you start with a strategic goal and work backward to achieve it, you should be able to establish a logical relationship between your intervention and the organizational outcome. I think there are ways for the chain to go awry, but the ultimate goal, in my mind, is creating an alignment between the behavior that the learning intervention is trying to establish, the change needed in the workplace, and the impact on the organizational outcomes.

The hot topic of return on investment (ROI) arises here. The general argument is that there should be a clear cost-benefit relationship for the investment in mobile. That argument is valid, but most ROI looks at a ratio of cost to benefit, which can be misleading. Consider that a mythical $1,000 investment might yield a $10,000 benefit, a 1,000 percent ROI. Would you really rather do that than a $200,000 investment that yields a $1M benefit? The ROI on the latter is only 500 percent, but the organizational benefit is much bigger! Focus on the largest organizational benefit, within the realms of reasonable expenditure.

Back in the analysis phase we talked about impacting metrics. At this point, you should be looking to see whether you have indeed impacted those metrics as much as you thought you could. If not, it is time to determine the reasons you are not having the desired impact and whether you need to tweak your solution, or whether to shut down the initiative. Of course, if you are impacting as you thought you were, or more so, it is time to leverage your success!

The issue previously raised in Chapter 8, the investment in a platform approach, also comes up here. Investments in specific developments to achieve a particular goal are straightforward to calculate. However, if you are being strategic and using each initiative to also develop infrastructure, that ongoing benefit may be worthwhile capturing. Do think strategically about building capability, not just immediate solutions, and look to justify those investments as well.

There is nothing unique to mobile here, at least when it comes to learnlets or performance support. The learning augment, however, may be harder to separate out from the overall experience. If you can compare an un-augmented course to an augmented one, you have a clear basis. Without such a baseline, however, the unique contribution of the mobile augment may be harder to establish, but should be valuable.

WE HAVE ISSUES HERE!

Little comes without attendant baggage, and mLearning is no different. Concerns about devices and access, accessibility, security, support, and more all arise. These issues cross legal, HR, and IT. Some general guidelines do exist.

Social Policies

As social media, we need to have rules around the use of mobile devices and some additional specifics as well. The discussion of social learning can be a target for executives concerned about employees frittering away valuable time or sharing internal secrets. While these concerns are legitimate, they can also be overblown.

The concern over socialization instead of work is not new to mobile devices. Many years ago, I was consulting to a company that was installing a new information technology infrastructure. The executives asked that email (a new capability at the time) not be enabled. The reasoning was that they did not want employees frittering away their time. Their people had phones, but somehow email was perceived to be "different."

Similarly, the concerns over people socializing are misplaced. If the workplace has a culture of sharing and mutual support, the conversations will be productive regardless of tool. On the other hand, if the culture is one in which people are not trusted and the management is controlling, irrelevant conversations and activities will occur with or without mobile devices. The rallying cry of my colleagues in the Internet Time Alliance is to provide the tools for productive dialog, and get the culture right. This holds true for mobile as well.

The goal should be to help employees understand what the needs are and to empower them to find the solution. As we have seen, the augmentation enabled by mobile devices is a powerful addition to organizational capability and should be eagerly adopted as another tool in the execution and innovation quiver, not as a concern for irrelevant activities.

In a similar way, the concern over sharing secrets via mobile devices really is not any different than sharing secrets using any other channel, including face to face, *as long as your users are aware of that.* Users may be ignorant of just how persistent and ubiquitous digital communications can be. What is shared can inadvertently or purposefully be shared more broadly and inappropriately.

The current spate of "sexting," whereby teens share inappropriate pictures of themselves, has prompted some serious consequences, and the ramifications may continue indefinitely. These days, anything posted on the web can live indefinitely, removed or not.

Further, it has been found that the lack of immediacy in asynchronous communication (read: email) can lead to surprisingly inappropriate behavior. Individuals have been ruder and more abrupt in email than they would be face to face.

In another way, people can inappropriately pass on information at parties, working on a train, or anywhere else. Just as the inappropriate behavior in conversations and on the phone can and should be made explicit and discussed, so too should policies around mobile communication. In many ways, it is just common sense: do not say anything on a phone or via IM or microblog or email that you would not say face to face.

IBM, for instance, has had social media policies that say, effectively, "Do not do anything in social media you would not do face to face" and that is true for mobile social as well. In short, be explicit about what appropriate behavior is across any medium, and ensure that it is also recognized as being relevant for mobile communications as well.

Accessibility

One real concern with mobile devices is the fact that various media are effectively unusable by some segment of the population. Blind users have trouble with graphics, deaf users may have a problem with audio files. And, of course, those with devices that cannot handle all formats may be unable to take advantage of particular forms of content or interactions.

There are two approaches here, and either is defensible. One is to ensure that all materials have an alternate representation: a transcript of an audio file, a text version of a diagram, and so on. This can be required by federal rules, or it can just be the *right* thing to do.

On the other hand, if the job aid or learning augment you are producing is not mandatory, and there is low overhead to produce a mobile-delivered version but much effort to create an alternative, you might consider that reaching those you can is better than not reaching anyone at all. Not everyone will have devices capable of all media, so you can either provide all the required devices, provide support to acquire any capability missed (such as providing a low cost MP3 player for those with only a PDA), or leave it to user discretion.

Naturally, if you require a particular capability or it disadvantages someone, you have a strong case to ensure there are all necessary variations. This is increasingly possible, both because tools make this easier and easier, and also because we are recognizing that a small amount of redundancy in development ensures a much greater flexibility in delivery.

Security

If IT block firewall access through the network, it is already being seen that individuals will surf the web through their phone connection. (Robert Gadd proposes that the new "cigarette break" is going outside for mobile access!) If IT provides access, they are creating more security holes for attackers to exploit. What is an IT group to do? And you *do* want to work well with them, for they can make things happen and may have budgets and tools as well as be an obstacle.

There are two major sources of concern about security: data on the device and data in transmission. If data is on the device or can be accessed through the device, and the device is mislaid or stolen (and this does happen), intellectual property can be comprised and a competitive advantage lost. Somewhat more difficult, but still doable, is the data being intercepted as it is transmitted.

There are solutions. Increasingly, handset manufacturers are providing hardware support for encryption and password locks for data. Third-party solutions also exist for securing the device, securing communications, remotely wiping devices that have gone missing, and even tracking down lost devices.

These require, however, the ability for the IT group to address the software issue. Machines running a Windows Mobile solution will have the easiest time, as Microsoft has positioned itself as the enterprise solution. Others have varying degrees of compliance.

A flip side is to make available access via a log-in only. The point here is not to detail all the solutions, which will change, but instead to identify characteristics of successful solutions.

You need to help IT recognize that the solution is not to try to control access, but instead to make sure that mobile use meets security and maintenance standards. To gain acceptance by IT, security will be critical. Several characteristics will be required of devices going forward:

- Passwords and remote wipe

- Encryption

- Digital certification

- Synchronization with enterprise software

- Ensuring conformance with the above

To Provide, or Not to Provide

Implicit in the previous discussions was a decision about whether to provide specific devices or merely make access available to individual devices. As always, there are tradeoffs. If you provide the device, you can take advantage of the specific capabilities of the device, managing security as well. Naturally, you also incur purchase, support, and management costs. If you only provide access, you do not have the cost or support issues, but you also have less flexibility in who and how you can support learning.

In one instance, a smartphone was provided as a PDA, but learners were able to insert their own SIM cards into the devices and then use them as phones as well, without the cost of the voice service to the organization. At Abilene Christian University, the organization provided a non-phone device *unless* the user agreed to pay for the phone service. The solutions can be as varied as the needs.

Support

Regardless of whether you provide the devices, there will be issues of support. If you provide the devices, there will be requirements for maintaining, updating, and assisting users with devices.

However, even if the devices are not provided by the organization, users can (and will) have issues with access, formats, restrictions, the other issues. Some devices will have problems with hardware and software limitations, other devices can have problems due to the network used (provider), and of course some users will just have problems.

A related issue is how to test solutions. With controlled devices, the testing is straightforward, although location issues may complicate the process. When making access generally available, it may be that certain common devices will be accepted (and tested for); otherwise the use is *caveat emptor.*

The last issue implies the topic of quality of service (QoS). When providing devices, a QoS will necessarily be established, but in the case of supported devices, the QoS may be dependent on factors out of the control of the responsible group. Clear decisions about what will be handled internally and what will be "your mileage may vary" will be important.

The take-home message of this chapter is, simply, that the problems are largely not unique to mobile, and solutions that have worked in other contexts transfer in relatively straightforward ways to solve mobile issues as well.

 QUESTIONS TO ASK

1. Have you developed your implementation plan?

2. Is your solution IT-compliant?

3. Do you have management and governance in place?

4. Have you established policies that provide sufficient guidance?

SECTION

LOOKING FORWARD

The mobile space is incredibly dynamic, and with increasing competitive pressures driving innovation, this is not going to change in the near future. Some of these changes will be evolutionary in nature, and some will be revolutionary. What should you be looking at and for?

You need to be strategic, recognizing the broader context of organizational learning and where mobile fits in. Then you also need to be aware of the significant changes that you can expect.

This final section includes the following chapters:

- Chapter 12. Being Strategic presents a performance ecosystem view of technology in organizational learning.
- Chapter 13. Trends and Directions covers current trends and likely convergences.
- Chapter 14. Get Going (Mobile) is a call to action.

CHAPTER

12

BEING STRATEGIC

Where does mobile fit in the bigger picture of organizational learning? Without recognizing the broad spectrum, it is hard to be strategic about when and where mobile learning makes sense.

Across a number of engagements with organizations around their use of technology to support execution and innovation, a pattern emerged that suggested some categories of activity that I have subsequently used effectively as a guide to strategic thinking.

THE PERFORMANCE ECOSYSTEM

The perspective is grounded in the realization that all learning is not formal, as we discussed earlier, and that there are a range of capabilities on the part of the learner. We also have several different contexts for digitally supported learning, both desktop and mobile, and we have individual and social learning. When we map out this space, we see that there are many potential areas where tools can augment performance. I call this perspective (seen in Figure 12.1) the *performance ecosystem.*

Note that the goal is not to use all the tools, but to ensure that all the niches are covered. And we want to do this in a systematic way so that, as we add capabilities, we do so in ways that build upon one another, creating a coherent and integrated whole, not a series

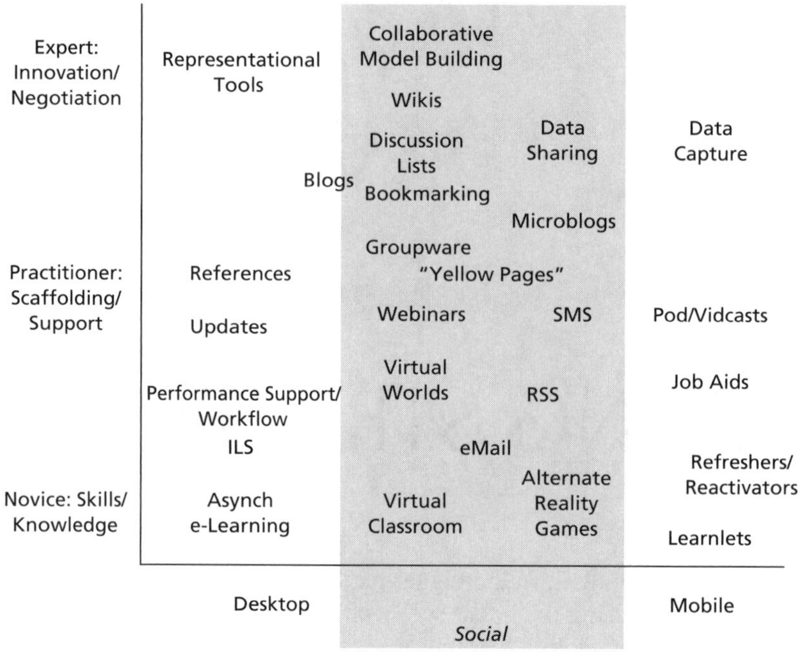

FIGURE 12.1. *The Performance Ecosystem*

of inconsistent functionalities. We do this by approaching eLearning strategically.

eLEARNING, STRATEGICALLY

Across the series of engagements, I saw that there were typically three starting or entry points (Figure 12.2) into using technology to support organizational performance: eLearning, performance support (via a performance focus), or eCommunity (social media, essentially). So offering courses online or hosting webinars was a typical entry point, as was having support tools and job aids available through portals or providing a way for discussions to occur and individuals to find expertise. Typically, however, these were done in an idiosyncratic fashion.

As stated in my chapter for *Michael Allen's eLearning Annual* (2009), I believe that organizations increasingly need to be agile to survive in an increasingly competitive environment. As a consequence, providing an integrated information environment is critical.

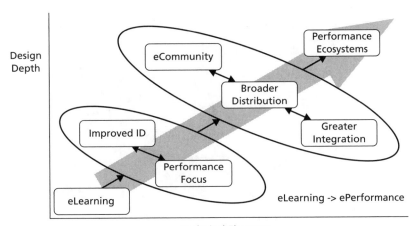

FIGURE 12.2.   *eLearning Strategy*

To do so, I extend the three components of eLearning, performance support, and eCommunity to include broader distribution (mobile) and greater integration (underpinning systems). I added in the recognition of a deeper instructional design because most eLearning is insufficiently informed of deeper learning. Until you recognize valuable components like challenge, emotional engagement, and more, you have no capability of appreciating learning designs that include things like gaming.

As discussed earlier, the benefits of greater integration, of developing a content model, are in efficiency, but greatly facilitate mobile delivery as well. However, choosing to develop a content strategy is more likely to yield benefits if it is done in conjunction with an awareness of the overall eLearning plan, as is mobile, performance support, eLearning, and eCommunity.

The Learner Perspective

Another way to look at it is from the learners' perspective. Do they see a confusing plethora of resources or a coherent environment in which to learn? My colleague Harold Jarche talks about the individual's "personal learning environment." Do your learners have such an environment, or instead are they facing a morass of incoherent technology tools? Your goal is to be considering how to create, from a learner

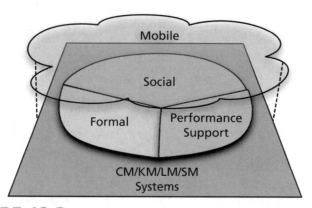

FIGURE 12.3. *Learner Performance Ecosystem*

perspective, a seamless environment for performance. See Figure 12.3 for one such system.

What the learner should see is an integrated infrastructure for formal learning, performance support, and social learning, built upon a foundation of content management, knowledge management, learning management, and social media systems. Mobile is a delivery layer on top of the environment, adding not only new channels but also new capabilities.

The goal here is not to explain a complete eLearning strategy, but to give you a context in which to consider a mobile initiative. In the long term, an eLearning strategy is a necessary component, but a mobile initiative should be considered in the context of the larger perspective of technology for organizational performance.

BEING OPPORTUNISTIC

Mobile does not happen in a vacuum. There are ongoing initiatives driven by IT, sales, operations, or HR. The question is, how can you take advantage of them? It can be hard to push mobile purely for learning, or even to push mobile by itself. What would be useful opportunities to capitalize on other endeavors?

The trick is to know the hooks. The leverage is that, for a small additional overhead, there is a potentially powerful additional outcome. Look for initiatives that are both a knowledge initiative, delivering or collecting information, or new technology deployments that might be easily mobile-enabled. Some initiatives and the associated opportunities include content management, knowledge management, wireless network installation, portal creation, and employee role or task categorization. Each of these has an associated rationale as to why mobile makes sense and the required effort to extend the initiative to mobile learning. Table 12.1 lists some of these opportunities.

If there is a content management system being installed, you should inquire as to whether mobile access is planned, and if none is, suggest that it could and should be. By having a repository for mobile content, you can add to it the content you wish individuals to have access to. Also find out whether users can upload content into the content management system and potentially argue for that capability. And find out how they plan to make content available and inquire about a mobile portal.

Similarly, if there is a portal initiative happening, inquire about whether the portals will be mobile-accessible, and if not, whether they can be. The ability to have content organized around communities, tasks, or other meaningful structures would be valuable for mLearning. Ideally, you would have representation on the portal process to help ensure that the portals are being used for learners, not for business units, or at least can be.

If a knowledge management initiative is underway, attempting to capture and share knowledge or to provide expertise location, having the resources mobile-accessible leverages that system to a broader audience and more contexts. Naturally, the concomitant activity is to make the initiative available through mobile devices.

On a related note, any social media initiative to allow people to communicate and collaborate provides an opportunity to suggest mobile enablement as well. Providing access to knowledge sharing is a positive component of a performance ecosystem.

If wireless networks are being installed, it suggests that even when you do not have a laptop with you, you could be productive through wireless device such as a smartphone or tablet. It may be worthwhile to lobby for enabling the wireless network to support a broad spectrum of devices.

If any other group is deploying mobile devices, for instance to facilitate communications among the sales team or to provide data

TABLE 12.1. Mobile Opportunities

Initiative	Mobile Opportunity	Rationale	Required Extension
Content Management	Delivery channel	Greater accessibility of content with marginal overhead	Add mobile format to content tool
Portals	Mobile access	Delivering performance support more broadly	Mobile-accessible versions
Knowledge Management	Broader distribution	Fuller access to knowledge when and where needed	Create mobile version
Social Media	Greater access	Ability to tap into and share knowledge	Mobile accessibility
Wireless Networks	Greater access	Facilitate broader access across devices	IT support
Mobile Devices	Leverage another unit's initiative	Marginal increase	Allow learning use

access to field service individuals, the opportunity exists to leverage that capability for further learning and performance needs. If nothing else, the opportunity to work with that initial endeavor can inform your further efforts to enable mobile across the organization.

By being strategic and opportunistic, your mobile initiatives have a greater likelihood for success, as will you.

 ## QUESTIONS TO ASK

1. Have you developed an ongoing eLearning strategy?

2. Have you considered the performers' "experience"?

3. Is mobile integrated into the larger eLearning strategy?

CHAPTER

13

TRENDS AND DIRECTIONS

As I have mentioned several times, the mobile space is dynamic. The devices continue to evolve, with the occasional revolution as well. The providers jockey for position, and platform players come and go.

Out of this chaos, however, some patterns and trends are emerging, and it is worth your time to understand these. Some of these are only possible, but all are probable.

MOBILE EXTENSIONS

One of the directions we are seeing is an increasing focus on mobile delivery. Tools, from learning management systems to webinar tools, are seeing mobile delivery extensions. For instance, Blackboard, a higher-ed focused learning management system, has a mobile interface, as do several virtual meeting tools.

The whole idea of sharing information between the mobile and desktop PIM is similarly being extended to other information applications. As mobile devices become more capable, particularly convergent devices, we are seeing that subsets of desktop applications are going mobile, including so-called "office" suites of word processing, presentation, and spreadsheet tools.

Similarly, several "sharing" tools that allow you to put information onto a hosted solution and access it from anywhere are creating mobile versions as well. Which brings us to the "cloud."

THE "CLOUD"

Where the data from those sensors would go is unknown, but in another sense it does not really matter. Increasingly, we do not have to know where our data is being sent or processed, as long as we have a connection to it. Products like Evernote take your data and store it out on the Internet, but the application handles the details and makes it available to you on many platforms. We say that the data is "in the cloud."

A more extreme version is web-based applications. In the cloud version of computing, websites provide the capabilities you used to expect would require dedicated applications on your computer. As a consequence, a very simple machine with a simple OS capable of running a web browser is all you need, and everything is done with an application implemented through the browser. While other companies have various versions of this, currently Google is pushing the envelope furthest, developing a streamlined and fast browser, Chrome, and a minimalist operating system (Chrome OS) to run the browser.

This lack of digital detail is the concept behind the cloud—that you do not have to worry about downloading and support the application nor where the data is, there is merely a way to access it independent of location.

The mobile implications are two-fold. First, your login details are all you need to work from anywhere. Any machine with a browser and connectivity is your computer. Second, you do not need a complicated device; all you need are a browser and an Internet connection, so that device can be local.

Michelle Lentz of WriteTechnology, a blogger on mobile devices (among other things), told me she "lives in the cloud." Essentially all her data and application use is Internet-based. Others, myself included, have some concerns over not having a local copy of our data. The recent example of a major provider and software partner losing the data for every user of a phone due to an operating error provides ample reason to be cautious.

There are organizational upsides and concerns over the cloud as well. One is whether the cloud is truly secure. Some organizations are arranging cloud-based servers, but run their own security on top of it. Of course, if the Internet connection goes, you are essentially unable to work. On the other hand, there can be lower expenditures on software and you are essentially outsourcing support to the application provider.

There is likely to be more cloud-based computing going forward. A recent research report from industry analyst firm Juniper Research, as reported by ReadWriteCloud (2010) put the number of enterprise mobile cloud workers at 130 million by 2014. Not insignificant numbers.

IMPACT

The benefits from mobile accrue, as the name suggests, from form-factors that allow easy portability. Consequently, there is a great desire to make things smaller and lighter, use lower energy, or more powerful in the same form-factor. Technology breakthroughs continue to happen that drive battery technology to greater performance, reduce power consumption requirements of processors, and add more capable memory.

One desire includes reducing the environmental footprint of mobile devices, which includes both the toxic waste produced in making or recycling mobile devices and also a reduction in the power required to manufacture and power these devices. Solar technologies are already appearing in chargers, and it is plausible that solar cells will appear on the devices themselves if they haven't already. In the developing world and remote locations, in particular, power from sources other than an energy grid could mean the difference between computational capabilities or none.

A new direction being pursued is *nanotechnology*, attempting to assemble materials at a molecular or even atomic level. The approach has promise for further miniaturization, including not just structural materials but also memory, processors, battery, and even charging capabilities.

There is every reason to believe that the devices will continue to become more powerful in capability as the technology advances increase.

SENSOR NETS

What if you had a lot of sensors, thousands or even millions, scattered across the country. You could aggregate that data into a dynamic picture. Well, many of these mobile devices *are* equipped with sensors. Not all are on all the time (for instance, the camera), but some are on at any time, pretty much (just as people are). What can we learn?

One of the new types of sensors is an accelerometer. What if there were an earthquake? Could we aggregate the accelerometer data to make a picture of the movement? Another type of sensor in some watches and dedicated GPS devices is a barometer. Barometric pressure is a big component of weather forecasting. Can we get a more accurate picture of weather fronts? Coupled with temperature information, it would be even more powerful.

I think that as sensor technologies shrink, we could include air quality monitoring, radiation, and more. With bandwidth and battery life increases, those sensors could be live and transmitting continuously, and we could have a much more detailed picture of the environment.

We could make GPS more accurate by correlating with known locations and data, or create virtual surveillance videos. By aggregating compass and GPS information, the direction a camera is facing could be coupled with others to record a location in 3D.

There are privacy concerns, of course, but overall the potential is fascinating.

GAMING TO GO

Having written a book on how to design learning games, a natural direction for me to explore is mobile gaming for learning. What is mobile gaming? and What is the learning potential?

Mobile gaming is becoming more sophisticated, not just on the handheld gaming platforms, but also on other devices. From "twitch" games (simple pattern-matching and reaction time games such as Pac-Man and Tetris), games have matured to include adventure, strategy, and other more cognitive genres.

These games are not context-specific but typically are used to occupy time when other activity is not available. The learning equivalent of the "twitch" games are the so-called "frame" games, where there is a knowledge-test framework (such as a quiz show template) into which any knowledge to be drilled can be inserted. The downside is that such templates tend to be overused due to learning objectives at too low a level.

As richer games appear, so too do the opportunities to do more meaningful games on handheld devices. Simulation-driven interactions were the core goal of my book *Engaging Learning: Designing e-Learning Simulation Games* (2005), and the same principles hold for mobile learning games.

The step from convenience to context-specific, however, provides a new opportunity. A mobile-specific type of game, *augmented reality games* (or ARGs), has the activity layered on top of real life, taking advantage of when and where you are to drive interaction. There are messages that may come in, via mobile or otherwise, that require decisions and actions. Moreover, environmental objects may play a role. In a game run to advertise a computer game, players around the country had to self-organize to get someone to a particular phone in a particular intersection in a particular city at a particular time to pick up a message with a clue necessary to advance the game!

The potential here for learning is immense. A simple example is having learners play a scavenger hunt game around the physical plant as an on-boarding process. For example, they might have to follow clues to find HR, the cafeteria, and their offices. You could layer on stories from the organizational lore, helping develop the cultural history. Or players could perform a simulated task in the real context before it really counts.

I assisted Jim Schuyler of Red7 Communications (see the examples for more) spreading an ARG around downtown Palo Alto, California, as a demonstration for the Institute for the Future. Players had to negotiate puzzles such as "Floodman's Torus" (Noah's Bagels) to rescue a stolen object.

If you have seen the movie *The Game* (and if you have not, I recommend it), you have seen the real potential. In the movie, the main character enrolls in a game where clues and the mystery soon start escalating: messages appear on nearby machines, strangers pass messages, and more. The point is that the game inserts itself into life.

I think that this form of learning has the potential to be more than effective, but to be truly transformational, and you should be primed to look for opportunities to take the learning experience to the "next level."

BLURRING BOUNDARIES

One of the recent technology advances has been in the area of virtual worlds (VW), where, through a computer-mediated interface, you enter and navigate around a 3D representation of a world. In this world, you can do things you cannot do in the real world, such as fly. The experience is much like so-called first-person shooter (FPS) computer games where you see through the character's eyes (or from slightly above and behind the character). Linden Lab's *Second Life* is the best-known example.

There are real advantages to virtual worlds. Karl Kapp and Tony O'Driscoll's recent book on 3D worlds, *Learning in 3D: Adding a New Dimension to Enterprise Learning and Collaboration* (2010) lays out the opportunities and possibilities nicely, with conceptual explanations and concrete examples detailing the benefits of immersive worlds when three dimensions are a component part of the learning requirements, and when social interaction can play a positive role in making the outcomes effective.

There are strong similarities between virtual worlds and augmented reality. In both cases, reality has been altered to make it more useful; it's just that one is virtual and one is real. The information presentation provides a nice integration of content and communication, and computation and capture can be delivered as well. In short, it's like the real world, only better.

The connection is only going to get stronger. Already, social networks are being made accessible by mobile (many regularly interact through mobile applications for Facebook, LinkedIn, and Twitter), and these capabilities will be extended to virtual worlds. The social connections of virtual worlds are now accessible outside of the world as well as "in world," and by the time you read this you will be able to navigate virtual worlds from your mobile device. It may be that your virtual world companions can join you in the real world, and vice versa.

SMART "PUSH"

One of the directions will come when we transition from Web 2.0 to Web 3.0. Web 1.0 was about what I call "producer-generated" content. It took resources or rare knowledge to be able to coordinate the content-development expertise to create a web page and manage a server to get it appropriately located and hosted to be seen.

Web 2.0 is about "user-generated" content and arose when web-based applications made it easy to generate content that could be web-hosted. Sites arose that allowed anyone to be sharing prose, photos, and even videos. Additional components include the 5-ables (as coined by Brent Schlenker of the eLearning Guild):

- *Searchable*: The content can be placed on the web where others can search for it.

- *Linkable*: The content can be pointed to by an URL, a link.

- *Taggable*: The content can be described (particularly by others, adding value) in ways that allow it to be found by particular terms.

- *Editable*: Others can improve the content or at least comment on it.

- *Subscribable*: You can indicate particular content that you want to track as it is updated or changed.

With these elements, user-generated content does not just exist, but can live in a virtuous cycle where it can be shared and improved upon, where it can have value added to it.

Web 3.0 is the next step (see Figure 13.1), and I believe it will be about system-generated content. Concepts such as Ontology Web Language (OWL), Resource Description Framework (RDF), and more provide the capabilities required. I do not necessarily mean systems composing unique content so much as systems combining data based on external information and serving it up under specific and semantic constraints.

Several examples are relevant here. I consider Wolfram Alpha, the computational search engine, to be an instance, as it takes your terms, parses them down, figures out the sources to use, and matches up the data to produce the answer for you. Amazon's recommendations also aggregate data from many users, and your personal record of purchases, to categorize you and figure out what other users you are like and what they have liked.

The reason I mention this is the possibility of using information about your tasks, your competencies and learning goals, your context, and/or your schedule to do custom content delivery. Using

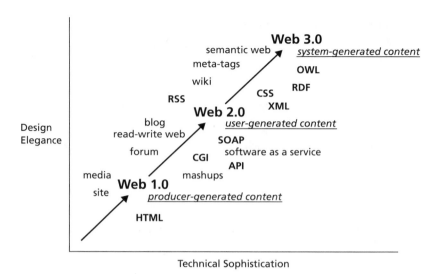

FIGURE 13.1. *Generations of the Web*

an intelligent engine with a set of rules, we could deliver the right information before a performance, during a performance, and/or after a performance to develop you as a learner across your life. (See Figure 13.2.)

So, for example, you could know that the user is currently learning about coaching and currently is working on developing a safe environment for sharing. Moreover, the person is in a supervisory role and has an upcoming coaching meeting. The system could review the specific learning goal beforehand, provide a reference sheet for the overall process, and then prompt for a review afterward (or connect the person to a mentor). Thus, the real performance becomes a learning opportunity.

The overall goal is to make the system a more effective partner, providing support as needed.

SLOW LEARNING

Inspired by the concept of slow food (a movement advocating taking time to search out local natural food, preparing it carefully, and enjoying it slowly), I have been interested in slow learning. Recognizing that natural learning is not an event, but a process that develops over time, the question is whether we can take a slower, more thorough

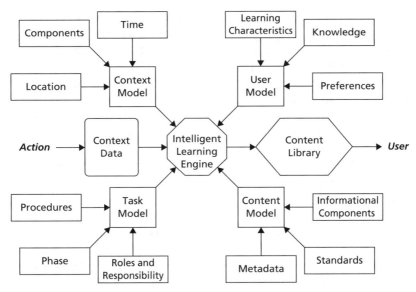

FIGURE 13.2. *Intelligent Learning Architecture*

approach to developing learners. This is what mentoring and coaching do in the real world. Can we do that with mobile? I believe we can.

As a metaphor, think of drip irrigation versus the typical watering paradigm, a flooding. Instead of a massive dump of information that will evaporate, how about just a little bit at a time, reinforced (spaced learning, as above). You can do this unintelligently, like drip irrigation, but you can do more. With some feedback from the learner, perhaps even some mass customization, and certainly with some empirical results, the system could move learners along at their own pace, augmenting the learners as they augment their lives.

With an intelligent architecture, clear definitions around our components, and some smart rules, I believe we could deliver custom learning. It may not be coming soon, but it can be done, and so it is easy to forecast that it *will* be done. This is not unique to mobile, but mobile provides a unique opportunity.

META-COGNITIVE MOBILE

The extreme of slow learning, developing the learners as we augment them, is to *meta-cognitively* augment the learners, developing not only their knowledge about specific domains, but also about their learning and themselves. The goal here is to look at their ability to manage time, to process certain types of information, at core to learn to learn and learn to perform, and augment it.

Imagine that we happen to know that learners are in a situation that they are uncomfortable in. We could just provide reassurances, but we could do more and provide rubrics for how to cope better. Whether it is an auditory presentation that they have trouble listening to, and we recommend diagramming the talk, or a social situation in which we provide some guidance on starting conversations, the system can focus on developing the learners as individuals, not just in the business skills they need for their current roles.

For instance, I have suggested elsewhere that it is a mistake to provide social media software to support collaboration, and then assume that learners are effective at learning socially. I believe we should make the skills explicit—and assess and develop them. Mobile delivery gives us a broader reach to do this in more contexts.

I think the limits we *should* be thinking about are not just taking the possibilities of mobile and pushing them to the utmost in helping us perform at our best, but helping us become the best we *can* be.

 ## QUESTIONS TO ASK

1. Are you tracking new developments?

2. Are you prepared to capitalize on changes?

CHAPTER

14

GET GOING
(MOBILE)

We have come a long way. I have tried to provide an overview of why we should be considering mobile, the foundational knowledge of technology and learning to ground the discussion, concrete examples of what can be done, principles about how to "think mobile," guidance on the mobile solution process, and a consideration of the bigger and longer-term picture. I hope I have achieved my goals and given you the tools to move forward.

There is only one last thing to do, and that is for you to get going!

You should by now be convinced that mobile is real—and doable. There is real value to be had, and the barriers are low enough that pretty much anyone can develop *some* mobile content. I hope you have also discovered there are opportunities for mobile to supplement your organizational goals in productive ways.

What I need you to do now is to go out and start a mobile learning initiative. Whether starting from the bottom-up with co-opted resources or recruiting support from above, it is time to take a serious step.

MOBILIZE!

Some of you will have already planned what need you will start with and how you will address it. Good for you. I wish you luck!

Some of you will have decided to start the discussion with peers and managers. I hope I have given you some ammunition, but there are more resources here, and will be at www.designingmlearning.com.

If any of you are hesitant, however, at least try this. Take your mobile device (or buy one), and push yourself out of your comfort zone. Try to find as many ways as you can to make yourself smarter with the mobile device. Try several of the ways to *think different* and apply it to yourself.

I am convinced that mobile will change the world. The ability to augment our capabilities in synergistic ways will empower us to new opportunities. It is up to us to harness this capability in useful ways. I hope that the information in this book gives you the leverage to start making the world a better place, but know that help is available should you need it.

Are you ready? Let's go mobile!

APPENDICES

A. BIBLIOGRAPHY

B. GLOSSARY

C. TOOLS

D. CHECKLISTS

APPENDIX

BIBLIOGRAPHY

Bozarth, J. (2010). *Social Media for Trainers.* San Francisco: Pfeiffer.

Carroll, J. (1990). *The Nurnberg Funnel: Designing Minimalist Instruction for Practical Computer Skill.* Cambridge, MA: MIT Press.

Clark, R., & Mayer, R.E. (2003). *e-Learning and the Science of Instruction: Proven Guidelines for Consumer and Designers of Multimedia Learning.* San Francisco: Pfeiffer.

Collins, A., Brown, J.S., & Holum, A. (1991). Cognitive apprenticeship: Making thinking visible. *American Educator, 12*(6), 38–47.

Collins, A., Brown, J.S., & Newman, S.E. (1989). Cognitive apprenticeship: Teaching the craft of reading, writing and mathematics. In L.B. Resnick (Ed.), *Knowing, learning and instruction: Essays in honor of Robert Glaser* (pp. 453–494). Mahwah, NJ: Lawrence Erlbaum Associates.

Cross, J. (2005). *Informal Learning: Rediscovering the Natural Pathways That Inspire Innovation and Performance.* San Francisco: Pfeiffer.

Cross, J., & Dublin, L. (2002). *Implementing e-Learning.* Alexandria, VA. ASTD Press.

eLearning Guild. (2007). *Mobile Learning 360 Research Report.* Santa Rosa, CA: eLearning Guild.

Gery, G. (1991). *Electronic Performance Support System.* Tolland, MA: Gery Performance Press.

IDC. (2010). More Than One Billion Mobile Workers Worldwide by Year's End, According to IDC. http://www.idc.com/getdoc.jsp?containerId=prUS22214110.

International Telecommunications Union. (2010). ITU sees 5 billion mobile subscriptions globally in 2010. http://www.itu.int/net/pressoffice/press_releases/2010/06.aspx.

Hutchins, E. (1995). *Cognition in the Wild.* Cambridge, MA: MIT Press.

ReadWriteCloud. (2010). How Many Enterprise Workers Will Work in the Mobile Cloud? Try 130 Million. http://www.readwriteweb.com/cloud/2010/03/how-many-enterprise-workers-wi.php.

Kapp, K., & O'Driscoll, T. (2010). *Learning in 3D: Adding a New Dimension to Enterprise Learning and Collaboration.* San Francisco: Pfeiffer.

Kirkpatrick, D. (1994). *Evaluating Training Programs.* San Francisco: Berrett-Koehler.

Metcalf, D. (2006). *mLearning: Mobile e-Learning.* Amherst, MA: HRD Press.

Morgan Stanley. (2009). The Mobile Internet Report. http://www.morganstanley.com/institutional/techresearch/mobile_internet_report122009.html.

Pink, D. (2005). *A Whole New Mind: Why Right-Brainers Will Rule the Future.* New York: Riverhead Press.

Pink, D. (2008). *The Adventures of Johnny Bunko: The Last Career Guide You'll Ever Need.* New York: Riverhead Press.

Quinn, C. (2005). *Engaging Learning: Designing e-Learning Simulation Games.* San Francisco: Pfeiffer.

Quinn, C. (2009). Populating the LearnScape: eLearning as Strategy. In M. Allen (Ed.), *Michael Allen's eLearning Annual.* Pfeiffer: San Francisco.

Rossett, A., & Schafer, L. (2007). *Job Aids and Performance Support: Moving from Knowledge in the Classroom to Knowledge Everywhere.* San Francisco: Pfeiffer.

Ruder Finn. (2010). New Study Shows "Intent" Behind Mobile Internet Use. http://www.prnewswire.com/news-releases/new-study-shows-intent-behind-mobile-internet-use-84016487.html.

Thalheimer, W. (2003). *Spacing Learning: What the Research Says.* Somerville, MA: Work-Learning Research.

APPENDIX

GLOSSARY

Affordance: A concept from user interface design, the term connotes the inherent capabilities provided by physical interaction, such as a most types of light switches "afford" changing a light state from on to off and vice versa. Visual interface elements can (and should) provide clues about how they can be acted upon, such as buttons being made to appear like pushable buttons in the world. Hidden affordances, capabilities that exist but are not obvious, such as dragging, require developing understanding of their use.

Augmented Reality: A situation where a device adds information onto the existing world. For example, the view through a camera can be augmented by information generated from knowing the location of the camera (via GPS) and direction of vision (internal compass). Similarly, auditory information can be triggered by proximity to add context such as historical information.

Augmented Reality Games (ARGs): Games that are played out across time, geography, and often across players. Typically, a player is navigating the real world and the game is laid on top of the activity, sending messages and providing clues that require decisions that trigger further consequences. They are a mix of mobile and game.

Bluetooth: A wireless technology and standard of short range that enables devices to talk to one another. Local devices can talk to mobile ones, or mobile devices can talk to one another (for instance, a mobile headset talking to a mobile phone).

Code Division Multiple Access (CDMA): One of two major standards for cell phone transmissions. Less used, globally, than GSM, CDMA has a strong position in the United States with carriers Sprint and Verizon.

Cell Phone: A mobile device including a phone and a limited set of core software (often including a browser), but usually unable to have applications added.

Global Positioning System (GPS): A U.S. military–developed system and standard for using satellite signals to triangulate location, providing accuracy to within several meters.

Global System for Mobile (GSM):   One of two major standards for cell phone transmissions. Prominent in Europe and globally, GSM is also a major system in the United States, with carriers T-Mobile USA and AT&T.

Haptic: A term used to cover all touch forms of interface, including keyboards, touch screens, vibration, and more.

Instant Messaging (IM):   A text chat mechanism between computers with a variety of standards, including ones propagated by Microsoft, Yahoo, AOL, and Skype.

iPod: Apple's music player that, coupled with the iTunes store, became an iconic point of reference for music players.

Local Area Network (LAN):   A term denoting a network covering a range from the size of a room to the size of a building, with distances in meters.

Microblogging: A form of text chat with the property that individuals can subscribe to receive all of another individual's messages. Twitter is the best-known example.

Operating System (OS):   The software that runs on a mobile device serving as a link between the hardware and the applications that communicate with the user. Different hardware can run the same operating system, and different operating systems might run on the same hardware, but applications typically must be rewritten to run on different operating systems.

Personal Area Network (PAN):   A network covering typically only a meter or so, often using Bluetooth.

Personal Digital Assistance (PDA):   A mobile device typically used to run PIM and user-chosen applications, but typically not including a phone.

Personal Information Management (PIM):   A suite of applications that assist individuals in managing their lives. Four core applications include contacts or addresses, a calendar for appointments, a way to take notes, and a way to save "to do" items.

Podcast: A voice file that can be saved to a mobile device with audio capabilities. The term originated with the iPod but has come to refer to all such audio files.

Portable Document Format (PDF):   A widely supported file format standard to share documents; typically handles text and static visuals (photos and graphics).

Proprioceptive: A term that captures your awareness of your own body. It is specifically used to represent the sense of knowing the relative position of your body parts, so that even with your eyes closed you can touch your nose.

QR Code: A standard for a 2D barcode, a QR code is a way to present a small amount of data such as some text, an URL, an email address, or a phone number so that a device such as a cell phone connected to a camera can take a picture and, with appropriate software, capture the text without typing.

Resolution: In device terms, refers to the dimensions of a screen in pixels, represented by a horizontal and a vertical pixel count. So, for example, a resolution of 320 x 240 is three hundred and twenty pixels by two hundred and forty pixels.

Retention: The term used to refer to the length of time some information is remembered. Used in learning as one of two goals for learning interventions, where the desire is for the intervention to last until the time it is needed.

Radio Frequency Identification (RFID): A standard communication protocol for technology that allows a small device to broadcast information to other neighboring devices.

Real Simple Syndication (RSS): A mechanism where a content stream from a source (e.g., a blog) can send signals that there is new content and that content can be aggregated for those who track that particular source.

Standard Courseware Object Reference Model (SCORM): A standard created by the Advanced Distributed Learning initiative of the United States government to support content interoperability.

Synch (Short for Synchronize): The way that applications on two different devices can combine their information. For example, if you have entered an event in your calendar on your mobile device, when next connected to your desktop device you can have that information synchronized onto your desktop, and vice versa.

Transfer: The term used to refer to information learned in one context to be relevant to another. Used in learning as one of two goals for learning interventions, where the desire is for the learning intervention to be applied to all appropriate contexts (and no inappropriate ones).

Universal Serial Bus (USB): A standardized data connection that allows a variety of devices to be connected to a computer, including peripherals (printers, keyboards), storage, and more.

User Interface (UI): The way in which an individual interacts with a digital device. For desktops, the UI is typically conveyed through the screen, in conjunction with a keyboard and a mouse. Mobile devices have a variety of interfaces, depending on their input and output devices.

Uniform Resource Locator (URL): A standard for the way in which to specify an Internet location. The most common one is a pointer to a web page, such as how http://www.quinnovation.com points to my website.

Virtual World: An immersive social environment in which you are represented by an "avatar" (a character that acts as your "agent" in the world) in a navigable 3D world and can interact with others. Linden Labs' Second Life is an example.

Voice over Internet Protocol (VoIP): A standard for delivering audio across the Internet, enabling telephone-style voice interaction.

Wide Area Network (WAN): A network that typically spans a much broader range, measured in kilometers or more. Cabled would be the Internet, wireless would be the cell phone data standards. New standards are emerging that may support wireless WAN access independent of cell phone connectivity.

Wi-fi: A standard that supports wireless Internet connectivity at about LAN distances and at a range of speeds.

APPENDIX

TOOLS

Mobile Category Opportunities

Role	Content	Capture	Compute	Communicate

Category by Formality

Formal	Informal
Content	
Capture	
Compute	
Communicate	

Media Opportunities

Role	
SMS	
Audio/Voice	
Documents	
Video	
Interactives	

APPENDIX

CHECKLISTS

Analysis

- ❑ What is the measure to impact?
- ❑ Is this a case for new skills or performance augmentation?
- ❑ What is the performance context?
- ❑ What are the task issues (for example, does the task require visual attention)?
- ❑ What is the audience device profile?
- ❑ What are the connectivity opportunities?
- ❑ Are there any limitations to your audience?
- ❑ Are there any limitations to mobile use:
  - ❑ Connectivity?
  - ❑ Screen size?
  - ❑ Input options?
  - ❑ Output options?
- ❑ What is the final learning objective?
  - ❑ Have you ensured it is about new behaviors, not just knowledge?

Design

☐ Is this a situation for:

> ☐ Content?
> ☐ Capture?
> ☐ Compute?
> ☐ Communication?

☐ Have you brought the right skills together for the team?

☐ Are you using a good design process?

☐ Have you set the right atmosphere for creativity?

☐ Are you using the right medium?

☐ Have you engaged the heart as well as the mind?

☐ Have you considered context specific options?

☐ Have you used good information design principles?

☐ Have you made a simple and consistent information architecture and navigation scheme?

☐ How can you minimize the solution?

☐ Have you considered cross-cultural issues?

Implementation

☐ Have you prototyped and evaluated your design?

☐ Have you looked for the most effective and efficient delivery mechanism?

☐ Do you have the necessary technology infrastructure?

☐ Do you have a plan for coping with technology changes?

☐ Do you have a messaging plan?

☐ Have you aligned rewards?

☐ Do you have stakeholders on board?

☐ Have you developed the necessary support structure?

☐ Have you put appropriate management and governance in place for your solution?

❏ Do you have appropriate policies and procedures in place?

❏ Have you considered accessibility?

Evaluation

❏ Do you have an evaluation plan?

❏ Do you know what metrics to measure?

❏ Do you have a data collection mechanism?

❏ Do you have a plan if things are going poorly, need improvement, or are going well?

ABOUT THE AUTHOR

Clark N. Quinn leads learning system design through Quinnovation, providing strategic solutions to Fortune 500, education, government, and not-for-profit organizations. Previously, he headed research and development efforts for Knowledge Universe Interactive Studio, and before that held executive positions at Open Net and Access CMC, two Australian initiatives in Internet-based multimedia and education. Clark is an internationally recognized scholar in the field of learning technology, with an extensive publication and presentation record, and has held positions at the University of New South Wales, the University of Pittsburgh's Learning Research and Development Center, and San Diego State University's Center for Research in Mathematics and Science Education. Clark earned a Ph.D. in cognitive psychology from the University of California, San Diego, after working for DesignWare, an early educational software company. Clark has maintained a consistent track record of advanced uses of technology, including mobile, social, performance support, adaptive learning systems, and award-winning online content, educational computer games, and websites. He an in-demand speaker as well as scholar, with a recent book, *Engaging Learning, Designing e-Learning Simulation Games*, and numerous articles and book chapters. He can be reached at: clark@quinnovation.com, +1–925–200–0881, blog.learnlets.com, and @quinnovator

INDEX

Page references followed by *fig* indicate an illustrated figure; followed by *t* indicate a table.

A

Abilene Christian University, 56, 170
Academic Advanced Distributed Learning (ADL) Co-Lab, 61
Accelerometers, 44, 46
Accessibility issues, 168–169
ADDIE design process, 134–137
Adobe Dreamweaver, 67
Adobe Flash, 154–155, 156
The Adventures of Johnny Bunko: The Last Career Guide You'll Ever Need (Pink), 119
Affective cognition, 24–25
Amazon: Kindle of, 38; search capabilities of, 189
AOL format, 47
Apple iPad, 39
Apple iPhones: description of technology, 35–36*fig*; higher education application of, 56. *See also* Cell phones
Apple iPods: description of technology, 33–34*fig*; development trends for, 40; higher education application of, 55, 56; museums and virtual tours using, 57
Apps (app stores): convergent model on, 41*fig*; types of, 46–47
Army Education Advisory Committee, 61
Ask Jeeves, 85
Asynchronous eLearning courses, 114
Audience response systems, 54
Audio: data delivery and, 117–118, 120*t*; information design and, 139; mobile design considerations for, 138, 139; MP3 files, 34; sensory channels for, 23*fig*–24
Audio recorders, 39
Augmentation: GPS system function of, 18–19, 123, 150; learning, 15–22, 27–28, 120–125, 146–147, 190–192; mLearning functions as, 17–19, 27–28; new emphasis on cognitive skills, 17–18.
See also mLearning augmentation functions; Performance support augment
Augmented reality: ARGs (augmented reality games), 187; mobile learning perspective of, 123; similarities between virtual worlds and, 188

B

Big 5 traits, 24
"Big Ideas," 91–92
BlackBerry: asynchronous eLearning courses on, 114; BES (BlackBerry Enterprise Server) platform, 8, 69; increased course completion rates using, 146; pharmaceutical sales use of, 66–67.
See also Cell phones
Blackboard, 183
Blogging, 102
Bluetooth, 48, 150
Bozarth, Jane, 100
BREW (Binary Runtime Environment for Wireless), 159
Brown, J. S., 110
Brown, Judy, 61–62, 65
Burn, Ken, 24
Buttons, 43

C

Cameras: Flip video, 39–40*fig*; QR codes (visual data encoding), 45*fig*–46; sensor function of, 44–45; trends in technology of, 40
Capture. *See* Media capture
Carroll, John, 125
CDMA (code division multiple access), 48–49
Cell phones:communication apps of, 47; expected growth of numbers, 3; mLearning applications using, 58–59; SMS (simple messaging system) of, 47, 49, 58, 117, 120*t*, 149; voice data

213

Cell phones: *(continued)*
delivery through, 117–118. *See also*
Apple iPhones; BlackBerry;
Smartphones
CellCast, 65
CellCast Server, 67
CellCast Widget, 67
Chrisman, Mark, 64, 100, 150
Chrome, 119, 184
Citysearch, 85
Civil War (PBS documentary), 24
Clark, Richard, 8
Clark, Ruth, 138
Clarke, Arthur C., 142
Cloud-based computing, 184–185
Cognition: affective and conative
components of, 24–25; distributed,
122–123; executive functioning guiding
tasks of, 16–17; media psychology
aspects of, 23*fig*–24; new emphasis on
developing skills of, 17–18. *See also*
Learning
Cognition in the Wild (Hutchins), 122
Cognitive Apprenticeship (Collins and
Brown), 110
Cognitive Apprenticeship model: core
activities using the, 111–112*fig*;
description of, 111; learning
components and mobile roles using,
113*fig*–114
Cognitive augmentation: GPS system as
example of, 18–19; meta-cognitive
mobile approach to, 191–192; mLearning
function as, 17–19, 27
Collins, A., 110
Comics, 118–119
Communication: apps capability of, 47;
audience response systems, 54; by
formality, 105; microblogging, 102–103;
mobile category opportunities for, 104*t*;
networking, 41*fig*, 47–49; as one of the
four C's of mobile capability,
101*fig*–103; output mechanisms
allowing, 41*fig*, 42–43
Communication channels: social networking
sites, 47, 102–103, 179, 180*t*, 188;
supporting mobile devices, 102
Compass, 46, 46. *See also* GPS (global
positioning system)

Compute: by formality, 105*t*; mobile
capability for, 100–101*fig*; mobile
category opportunities for, 104*t*
Conative cognition, 24–25
Concepts: application of, 121–122;
elaboration of, 121; mobile design
augmenting formal learning of, 146–147;
mobile design presenting the, 145–146;
personalization of, 120–121. *See also*
Information
Conceptually dynamic information, 23*fig*
Conceptually static information, 23*fig*
Conference presentation recording, 57–58
Confirmation bias, 141
Conner, Marcia, 103
Content: checking accuracy of captured,
163; design considerations for, 139;
designing Sports Byte STEM education,
78–80; intellectual property ownership
of, 163; interactive nature of mLearning,
10; microcourses or more modular,
114–115; as one of four C's of mobile
capability, 99*fig*; push versus pull for
learning, 124–125, 149; Service Magic
learning, 85–88; Web 1.0
producer-generated, 188; Web 2.0
user-generated, 188; Web 3.0
system-generated content, 189; working
with smaller chunks of knowledge for,
140; "writing for the web," 137–138.
See also Information
Content management initiative, 179, 180*t*
Content tools, 157–159
Context: contextually static information,
23*fig*; contexual dynamic information,
23*fig*; contextualization of information,
121; as king in mobile design, 149–150
Convergent model: apps, 41*fig*, 46–47;
illustrated diagram of, 41*fig*; input, 41*fig*,
43–44; networking, 41*fig*, 47–49; output,
41*fig*, 42–43; portable platform, 41*t*, 42;
QR codes, 45*fig*–46; sensors, 41*fig*,
44–46
Copyright issues, 163
Cross, Jay, 25, 29, 123, 124, 162
Cross-platform development, 159–160
CSS, 154
Custom programming, 9, 159–160
Cyberspark.net, 88

D

Data delivery: documents, 120*t*;
interactives, 119, 120*t*; media and,
118–119; media opportunities for,
119–120*t*; podcasts or audio/voice,
117–118, 120*t*; SMS (simple messaging
system), 47, 49, 58, 117, 120*t*; video,
120*t*. *See also* Mobile delivery
Design. *See* Mobile design
DesignWare, 88
Development. *See* Mobile development
Digital video recorders, 39–40*fig*
Distributed cognition, 122–123
DITA (Darwin Information Typed
Architecture) platform, 71, 72–73, 154,
157
Document media, 120*t*
Double double P's, 142–143
Dublin, Lance, 162
Duke University, 56
DVDs, 34

E

*e-Learning and the Science of Instruction:
Proven Guidelines for Consumer and
Designers of Multimedia Learning* (Clark
and Mayer), 138
E-learning SCORM standards, 61, 70
Earphones, 43
Egoless design, 141
Elaborating conceptual information, 121
eLearning: learner's perspective of,
177–178*fig*; strategic approach to,
176–177*fig*
eLearning Guild: Devlearn conference
(2009) of, 70; mLearning as defined by,
4, 38; mobile application demonstration
by, 57; Research Report (2007) by, 131
Electronic Performance Support Systems
(EPSS), 26
*Engaging Learning: Designing e-Learning
Simulation Games* (Quinn), 25, 131, 187
eReaders, 38–39
Evaluating Training Programs
(Kirkpatrick), 165
Evaluation: Kirkpatrick's four levels of,
165; process of, 164, 165–166;
qualitative data used in, 165; ROI (return
on investment) issue of, 166; tracking

and reporting usage, 164–165. *See also*
Mobile implementation
Evernote, 184
Evite, 85
Evolutionary prototyping, 142–143
Ewing Marion Kauffman Foundation, 76,
80
Executive functioning: digital devices
augmenting, 16*fig*–17; distribution of
tasks guided by, 16–17
Expertise factor, 141

F

Facebook, 47, 87, 102, 188
Federal Express, 56
Firewalls, 169
First-person shooter (FPS) computer games,
188
5-ables of Web2.0, 189
Flash, 154–155, 156
Flip video camera, 39–40*fig*
"Floodman's Torus" (Noah's Bagels) [ARG
game], 187
For Inspiration and Recognition of Science
and Technology (FIRST), 80
Formal learning: augmentation of, 19–20;
comparing informal and, 26*fig*; mobile
capability opportunities for, 104, 105*t*.
See also Learning
Formal learning augment: Cognitive
Apprenticeship model of, 110–114;
description of, 19–20; microcourses or
minimalist approaches to, 114–115;
mobile design as, 146–147
Format standards, 153–155
Four C's of mobile capability: capture as,
99–100*fig*, 104*t*–105*t*; communicate as,
101*fig*–103, 104*t*–105*t*; compute as,
100–101*fig*, 104*t*–105*t*; content as,
99*fig*, 104*t*–105*t*; introducing the,
98–99; issues of delivering, 156–160;
learning roles/levels applications of,
103–104
Functional fixedness, 141

G

Gadd, Robert, 65, 132, 169
Game Boy, 36
The Game (film), 187

Games: expansion to mobile, 186–187; first-person shooter (FPS), 188; handheld, 36–37*fig*; learning potential of mobile, 187

Gery, Gloria, 26

Global mLearning applications, 58–59

GoKnow software, 83

Google Goggles, 100

Google Maps, 19

Google's Chrome, 119, 184

Governance: definition of, 163; mobile implementation role of, 163–164

GPS (global positioning system): augmentation role of, 18–19, 150; augmenting reality using, 123; barometer sensor in, 186; data capture by, 99; sensor function of, 44; trends in technology of, 40. *See also* Compass

Graffiti (graphic input language), 32

GSM (global system for mobile), 49

H

H.263 format, 156

H.264 format, 156

Handheld gaming: Leapster, 37; Nintendo DS, 36, 37*fig*; technology of, 36

Hart, Jane, 123

Hashtags, 102–103

Hawkins, Jeff, 30

Healthcare organizations: AIDS education through mobile devices, 58; mobile devices for information systems of, 56

Hermeneutic philosophy, 115*fig*–116*fig*

Higher education mLearning applications, 55–56

Horn, Bob, 139

Hot Lava Software, Inc., 76, 79

HSN, 85

HTML 5, 155

HTML, 154

Human performance technology (HPT) model, 134–135

Husband, Jon, 123

Hutchins, Ed, 122

Hybrid Learning Systems, 70–74, 97, 157

I

IAC/InterActiveCorp, 85

IBM social media policies, 168

IDC, 8

IM (instant messaging), 47. *See also* SMS (simple messaging system)

Immersive Learning Technologies Team, 61

Implementation. *See* Mobile implementation

Implementing eLearning (Cross and Dublin), 162

INATT (it's not about the technology), 29

"Inert knowledge," 21

Informal Learning: Rediscovering the Natural Pathways That Inspire Innovation and Performance (Cross), 25, 124

Informal learning: comparing formal, 26*fig*; exploring methods of, 25–27; mobile capability opportunities for, 104, 105*t*; mobile support of, 123–124. *See also* Learning

Information: advantages of intelligent search engine for, 189–190; augmenting process of learning, 15–22; elaborating conceptual, 121; EPSS principle of providing support of learning, 26; "media psychology" of processing media, 23*fig*–24; as performer support component, 116*fig*; personalization of, 120–121; proprioceptive, 23. *See also* Concepts; Content

Information architecture, 139–140

Information design, 139

Information mapping, 139

Infrared Data Association (IrDA), 48

Infrared technology, 48

Input: convergent model on, 41*fig*; types of, 43–44

Institute for the Future (Palo Alto), 187

Intellectual property, 163

Intelligent learning architecture, 191*fig*

Interactivity: data delivery, 119, 120*t*; Flash, 154–155; mLearning, 10

Interface design, 139–140

International Telecommunications Union, 3

Internet: advantages of intelligent search engine, 189–190; Google search engine capabilities, 19, 100, 119, 184; Web 1.0, 188, 190*fig*; Web 2.0, 47, 87, 102–103, 179, 180*t*, 188, 190*fig*; Web 3.0, 189–190*fig*; Wolfram Alpha search engine, 189. *See also* Mobile Internet

Internet Time Alliance, 103, 123, 167

Interviews: David Metcalf, 95–96; Judy Brown, 61–62
iPods. *See* Apple iPods
iStore (software), 34
iTunes University, 34, 55

J

Jarche, Harold, 123, 177
Java, 155
Java ME (Java Mobile Edition), 159
Jennings, Charles, 123
Job Aids and Performance Support (Rossett and Schafer), 110, 147
Jogdials (or trackwheels), 44
Junior Engineering Technical Society, 80
Juniper Research, 185

K

K12 education: adapting mobile devices for, 54–55; audience response systems used for, 54; benefits of contextual applications for, 53–54; convenience aspects of mobile devices for, 54; designing mLearning context for, 52, 53; handhelds used for, 52–53; St. Mary's City Schools (SMCS) use of mLearning, 81–85; SMS quizzes, 76, 77*fig*, 80; Sports Byte STEM education via mLearning, 76–81
Kapp, Karl, 188
Katz, Heather A., 76
Kaufmann Foundation, 76–77, 80
Keyboards, 44
Keypads, 43
Kindle, 38
Kirkpatrick, Donald, 165
Kirkpatrick's four levels of evaluation, 165
Kitchen sink analysis, 142
Knowledge: "inert," 21; working with smaller chunks of, 140. *See also* Learning
Knowledge management initiative, 179, 180*t*
Knowledge Universe Interactive Studio, 88
Knowledge-dump, 20, 21
Kovalik, S., 79

L

LAN (local area networks), 48
Laptops, 38

LeapFrog, 37
Leapster, 37
Learner performance ecosystem, 178*fig*
Learners: eLearning from perspective of, 177–178; performance ecosystem of, 178*fig*; support issues related to, 170–171
Learning in 3D: Adding a New Dimension to Enterprise Learning and Collaboration (Kapp and O'Driscoll), 188
Learning: EPSS principle of providing support of, 26; intelligent learning architecture for, 191*fig*; knowledge dump and, 21; mLearning as being about performance and, 18–19; mLearning roles in augmenting, 27–28; mobile capability opportunities for, 104, 105*t*; mobile gaming and potential for, 186–187; push versus pull, 124–125, 149; service, 54; seven C's of, 20; "slow," 190–192; social, 27; spaced practice effects for, 108, 109*fig*; two-fold goals for effective, 22. *See also* Cognition; Formal learning; Informal learning; Knowledge
Learning augmentation: adding motivation, 27; application of concept, 121–122; distributed cognition, 122–123; elaboration of concept, 121; extending learning processes, 28; "least assistance principle" of, 125; meta-cognitive mobile, 191–192; personalization and contextualization, 120–121; process of, 15–22; of slow learning, 190–192; supporting learner preferences, 28; taking advantage of contextual opportunities, 28
Learning management systems (LMS): Blackboard's mobile interface, 183; existing platforms connecting mobile via, 131; mobile device integration with, 164–165. *See also* Management
Learnlet approach: to content minimalism, 114–115; mobile design using, 143–146
Learnlet minimalism approach, 114–115, 143–144
Learnlets (blog), 114–115
"Least assistance principle": as minimalism basis, 125; mobile design, 148–149
LendingTree, 85
Lentz, Michelle, 184

Lights, 42
Linden Labs, 37
Linguistic information, 23*fig*–24
LinkedIn, 47, 102, 188
Ludwig, Barbara, 129, 131, 164

M

McAffee, Andrew, 131
McCloud, Scott, 119
Management: definition of, 163; initiative
  for content, 179, 180*t*; initiative for
  knowledge, 179, 180*t*; mobile
  implementation role of organization,
  163–164. *See also* Learning management
  systems (LMS)
MapQuest, 19
MASIE Consortium, 61
Mayer, Richard, 138
Media: comics, 118–119; data delivery,
  118–119; document, 120*t*; mobile design
  matching message with, 149; properties
  of, 23*fig*–24; social, 47, 102–103, 179,
  180*t*, 188
Media capability, 28
Media capture: apps available for, 47; by
  learning formality, 105*t*; mobile
  capability for, 99–100*fig*; mobile
  category opportunities for, 104*t*; mobile
  devices used for, 54. *See also* Capture;
  Media capture
Media controls design, 138
Media opportunities: documents, 120*t*;
  interactives, 119, 120*t*; podcasts or
  audio/voice, 117–118, 120*t*; SMS
  (simple messaging system), 47, 49, 58,
  117, 120*t*; video, 120*t*
Media players: Apple iPod, 33–34*fig*;
  iStore and iTunes University innovations,
  34; technology of, 33–35
"Media psychology," 23*fig*–24
Media viewers, 47
Meta-cognitive mobile, 191–192
Metcalf, David, 15, 74, 95–96, 148
Michael Allen's eLearning Annual (Allen),
  176
Micosoft formats, 154, 156
Microblogging, 102–103
Microcourses, 114
Microphones, 46
MicroSD card, 48

Miller, Joe, 37
Minimalism: learnlet approach to content,
  114–115; learnlet approach to design,
  143–146; "least assistance principle"
  basis of, 125; synergy between Zen of
  Palm and, 137
Mixed Emerging Technology Integration
  Lab (METIL), 74
mLearning: as being about learning and
  performance, 15–19; capabilities of, 4;
  definition of, 4–5; making the business
  case for, 10–12; misconceptions about,
  8–10; trends and directions for,
  183–192; why it time for, 1–2. *See also*
  Opportunistic strategy
mLearning application examples: Hybrid
  Learning System for flexible delivery,
  70–74; METIL for multiplatform mobile
  simulation/game templates, 74–76;
  pharmaceutical sales, 65–70; Red7 vision
  of ubiquitous learning experiences,
  88–93; St. Mary's City Schools
  (SMCS), 81–85; Service Magic
  learning content, 85–88; STEM
  education, 76–81; T-Mobile for learning
  augment, 64–65
mLearning applications: feasibility of
  courses, 9; global perspective on, 58–59;
  higher education, 55–56; for K12
  learning, 52–55, 76–85; nonformal,
  57–58; organizational, 56–57
mLearning augmentation functions: as
  cognitive augment, 17–19, 27, 191–192;
  performance support augment, 28; roles
  as learning augment, 27–28. *See also*
  Augmentation
mLearning courses: feasibility of, 9;
  learnlet approach to, 114–115, 143–146;
  "least assistance principle" basis of, 125,
  148–149; selected organization examples
  of, 56–57, 64–93; synergy between Zen
  of Palm and minimalism for, 137
mLearning (Metcalf), 15, 148
MMS (multimedia messaging system), 49
Mobile accrue, 185
Mobile capability opportunities: categories
  by formality, 104, 105*t*; categories of,
  103–104*t*; context over convenience,
  106–107; custom stage of, 106–108;
  proactive stage of, 105–106; reactive

stage of, 104–105; for specific initiatives, 178–180*t*

Mobile delivery: MDTS (Mobile Delivery and Tracking System), 79; sensor nets, 186; SMS (simple messaging system), 47, 49, 58, 117, 120*t*; trends in extensions of, 183–184. *See also* Data delivery

Mobile design: ADDIE design process for, 134–137; generalities for, 137–143; resolution and, 140; specifics for, 143–150; taking on a mobile initiative for, 150; taking a platform approach to, 129–132; WIIFM (What's in It for Me) aligning meaning into, 144; "Zen of Palm" guiding, 125–126, 137

Mobile design generalities: design process traps, 141; design rubrics, 141–143; formal learning augment, 146–147; information design, 139; interface design and information architecture, 139–140; Learnlet approach to minimalist design, 143–146; "least assistance principle," 148–149; less is more, 137; media for mobile, 137–139; performance support augment, 147–148

Mobile design specifics: formal learning augment, 146–147; learnlet approach, 143–146; not right answers, only tradeoffs, 143

Mobile development: content models for, 157–159; content tools for, 157; custom programming, 159–160; delivering capability issue of, 156–160; mobile Web and, 157; standard formats issue of, 153–155, 156

Mobile device applications: global perspective on, 58–59; higher education, 55–56; for K12 learning, 52–55; mLearning examples of, 64–93; nonformal, 57–58; organizational, 56–57

Mobile devices: augmenting performance using, 16*fig*–17; definition of, 4–5; function as learning devices, 7; growth and capabilities of, 3–4; making the business case for mLearning and, 10–12; misconceptions about organizational provision of, 9; mLearning available through variety of, 10; mobile opportunities for leveraging another unit, 179, 180*t*, 181; standard formats for, 153–155, 156; typical everyday uses of, 5–6; ways to get the most out of, 97–98

Mobile devices technology: an Apple iPhone, 36*fig*; an Apple iPod, 34*fig*; cloud-based, 184–185; convergent model of, 41*fig*–49; digital video and audio recorders, 39–40; flip video camera, 39–40*fig*; handheld gaming, 36–37; increasing portability, 185; media players, 33–35; mobile phones, 32–33; nanotechnology, 185; Nintendo DS, 37*fig*; Palm Pilot, 30–32; PalmOS PDA, 30*fig*; push, 124–125, 149, 188–190*fig*; Smartphone, 35; tablets, netbooks, and eReaders, 38–39; trends in developing, 40–41; a typical cell phone, 33*fig*

Mobile gaming: ARGs (augmented reality games), 187; description of, 186; handheld, 36–37*fig*; learning potential of, 186–187

Mobile implementation: accessibility issue of, 168–169; management and governance impact on, 163–164; organizational change and, 162–163; planning for, 161–162; providing support issue of, 170–171; security issues of, 169–170; social policies issue of, 167–168. *See also* Evaluation

Mobile Internet: cloud-based, 184–185; increasing growth and use of, 7–8. *See also* Internet

Mobile models: augmented reality using, 123, 187, 188; categories of opportunities for using, 104–108, 120*t*; data delivery using, 117–119; distributed cognition using, 122–123; elaborating concepts for learning using, 120–122; four C's of mobile capability, 98–104; frameworks for using, 108–115; informal learning using, 123–124; "least assistance principle" of support from, 125; performer support using, 115–117; push versus pull for learning content using, 124–125, 149; spaced practice for learning, 108; ways to get the most out of, 97–98; "Zen of Palm" guiding use of, 125–126, 137

Mobile phones, cell phones, 32–33*fig*

Mobile Web, 157

Morgan Stanley, 7
MP3 players: audio files of, 34; format of, 154; Magic Services mLearning delivery on, 87; museums and virtual tours using, 57; standard format of, 156; technological development of, 34
MP4 (video), 34, 156
MPEG-4, 156
MSN format, 47
Museums: mobile devices used in, 57; Yerba Buena Center for the Arts (YBCA) "Big Ideas," 91–93

N

Nanotechnology, 185
Netbooks, 38–39
Networking: convergent model on, 41*fig*; description and types of, 47–49
Newcomb, Scott, 81
Newman, F. M., 79
Nielsen, Jakob, 137–138
Nintendo DS, 36, 37*fig*
No limits analysis, 142
Nonformal mLearning applications, 57–58
Norris, Cathie, 53
The Nurnberg Funnel: Designing Minimalist Instruction for Practical Computer Skill (Carroll), 125

O

O'Driscoll, Tony, 188
Office of Learning and Information Technology (OLIT), 61
OnPoint, 157
OnPoint Digital, 65, 132
Ontology Web Language (OWL), 189
Opportunistic strategy: for mobile capacity by formality, 103–108; mobile opportunities for specific initiative, 178–180*t*; for using selected media, 120*t*. *See also* mLearning; Strategic thinking
Organizations: mLearning applications in selected, 56–57, 64–93; mobile devices used by healthcare, 56, 58; mobile implementation and characteristics of, 162–164; mobile opportunities for specific initiative, 178–180*t*; mobile trends and directions for, 183–192; moving toward mobilization, 193–194;

opportunities for mobile capacity by learning formality, 103–108; opportunities for using selected media, 120*t*; support issues and decisions by, 170–171
OS (operating system): Chrome, 119, 184; issue of proprietary, 155; Palm Pilot, 30*fig*, 31, 32. *See also* Platforms
Output: convergent model on, 41*fig*; types of, 42–43
OutStart, 76, 157

P

Palm Pilot, 30–32
PalmOS PDA, 30*fig*
PAN (personal area networks), 48
Patten, B., 79
PDAs (personal digital assistants): used for K12 education purposes, 52–53; museums and virtual tours using, 57; Smartphone expansion of, 35–36*fig*; technology of, 30*fig*–31
PDF (portable document format), 156
Pedagogy: on facilitating effective learning, 22; mobile augmenting formal learning with enlightened, 19
Performance: augmenting process of, 15–16*fig*; GPA (global positioning system) as support of, 18–19; learner performance ecosystem, 178*fig*; mLearning as being about learning and, 17–19
Performance ecosystem, 175–176*fig*
Performance support augment: application of concept for, 121–122; communication, 28; considering performer needs for, 115, 116*fig*; data and processing ability, 28; distributed cognition for, 122–123; elaboration of concepts for, 121; EPSS principle of providing learning and, 26; GPS (global positioning system) as, 18–19, 150; Hermeneutic philosophy on "action in the world" for, 115*fig*; "least assistance principle" of, 125, 148–149; media capability, 28; mLearning augmentation role in, 28; mLearning framework for, 108, 110; mobile design as, 147–148; mobile models for, 115–117; personalization and contextualization for, 120–121; planners

and sidekicks categories of, 110. *See also* Augmentation

Personalization of information, 120–121

Personnel Decisions Research Institute, 76

Pharmaceutical sales, 65–70

PhoneGap, 74

PIM, 47, 183

Pink, Dan, 17, 119

Pink Yourself, 92

Planners, 110

Platforms: connecting existing LMS via mobile, 131; convergent model on, 41*fig*; cross-platform development, 159–160; Darwin Information Typed Architecture (DITA), 71, 72–73; description of, 42; DITA (Darwin Information Typed Architecture), 71, 72–73, 154, 157; proprietary OS running different, 155; smartphone, 159; standard formats for, 153–155, 156; understanding mobile as a, 129–132. *See also* OS (operating system)

PlayStation Portable (PSP), 36

Podcasts: technology of, 34; voice data delivery through, 117–118, 120*t*

Portal initiative opportunity, 179, 180*t*

Postpone programming, prefer paper, 143

Premature evaluation, 141

Projection, 42

Proprioceptive information, 23

Pull technology, 124–125, 149

Push technology: moving toward smart Web 3.0, 188–190*fig*; pull versus, 124–125, 149; SMS as, 149

Q

QoS (quality of service), 171

Qualcomm, 129, 131, 159, 164

Quinnovation QR code, 45*fig*–46

R

Radio frequency identification (RFI), 46

Re-applying concept, 147

Re-conceptualize, 146

Re-contextualize, 146–147

ReadWriteCloud, 185

Real Simple Syndication (RSS) standard, 34

Recorders, 39–40*fig*

Red7 Communications, 88–93, 187

Reporting usage, 164–165

Research in Motion's BlackBerry series, 35

Resolution, 140

Resource Description Framework (RDF), 189

Revolutionary prototyping, 142

Rockwell, Kris, 70, 97, 154, 157

ROI (return on investment), 166

Rossett, Allison, 108, 110, 147

Ruder Finn, 7

RWD Technologies, 74

S

St. Marys City Schools (SMCS), 81–85

Sánchez, A. I., 81

Sanregret, Bob, 58, 76

Schafer, Lisa, 110, 147

Schlenker, Brent, 189

Schone, B. J., 129, 131, 164

Schreck, Gina, 85

Schuyler, Jim "Sky," 88–89, 187

SCORM standards, 61, 70

Screens, 42

SD card, 48

Search engines: advantages of intelligent, 189–190; Google capabilities as, 19, 100, 119, 184; Wolfram Alpha, 189

Second Life, 87

Security issues, 169–170

Selker, Ted, 43

Sensor nets, 186

Sensors: convergent model on, 41*fig*; sensor nets, 186; types of, 44–46

Service learning, 54

Service Magic, 85–88

Set effects, 141

Seven C's of learning, 20

Sidekicks, 110

SIM (subscriber identify module) card, 49

Skype, 47

Slow learning: intelligent learning architecture supporting, 191*fig*; meta-cognitive mobile to support, 191–192; moving toward concept of, 190–191

Small screen issue, 9

Smartphones: description of technology, 35–36*fig*; organizational uses of, 57; platforms for, 159. *See also* Cell phones

SME model of negotiation, 148–149
SMS quizzes: STEM education use of, 76, 80; template for, 77*fig*
SMS (simple messaging system): data delivery using, 117, 120*t*; global use of, 58; as "push" technology, 149; technology of, 47, 49. *See also* IM (instant messaging)
Social learning, 27
Social media: mobile opportunities for, 179, 180*t*; technology and mobile devices supporting, 47, 102–103, 188
Social Media for Trainers (Bozarth), 100
Social networking: Facebook, 47, 87, 102, 188; LinkedIn, 47, 102, 188; mobile devices supporting, 102–103, 188; mobile opportunities for, 179, 180*t*; technology supporting, 47; Twitter, 47, 102–103, 188
Social policies, 167–168
Sociocultural elements, 141
Software development kits (SDKs), 159
Soloway, Elliot, 37, 52–53
Spaced practice effects, 108, 109*fig*
Spacing Learning: What the Research Says (Thalheimer), 108, 109
Speakers, 42
Sports Bytes (STEM-themed curriculum), 78–81
Standard formats, 153–155, 156
STEM education: challenge of mobile delivery of, 77–78; designing mobile content and delivery of Sports Byte, 78–80
Strategic thinking: eLearning strategy, 176–178*fig*; performance ecosystem, 175–176*fig*. *See also* Opportunistic strategy
Subject-matter experts (SMEs), 21
Support issues: to provide specific devices or not, 170; QoS (quality of service), 171; testing solutions and providing support, 170–171
Systematic creativity, 142

T

T-Mobile USA, 64, 100, 150
T-Mobile USA Training and Development, 64

Tablets, 38–39
Tactile category, 43
Task by percentage improvement, 12
Team design, 141
Telecommunting, estimates on, 8
Thalheimer, Will, 108, 109
three strategies design, 142
Tillett, Jeff, 64, 100, 150
Touchscreens, 43
Trackball, 44
Tracking usage, 164–165
Trackwheels (or jogdials), 44
Trends: cloud-based computing, 184–185; meta-cognitive mobile, 191–192; mobile accrue, portability, and nanotechnology, 185; mobile extensions as, 183–184; mobile gaming, 186–187; moving toward smart "push" technology, 188–190*fig*; sensor nets, 186; slow learning, 190–191*fig*; virtual worlds (VW), 188
"21st Century Skills," 17
Twitter, 47, 102–103, 188

U

Universal serial bus (USB), 48
University of Central Florida, 74
University of Michigan, 52
University of North Texas, 53
University of Wisconsin System Administration, 61
U.S. Department of Defense, 61
U.S. Department of Defense Board Agency Announcement (BAA), 70–71

V

Vibration, 43
Video: data delivery using, 120*t*; digital video recorders, 39–40*fig*; Flip video camera, 39–40*fig*; information design and, 139; media opportunities for using, 120*t*; mobile design considerations for, 138; MP4, 34, 156
Virtual tours, 57
Virtual worlds (VW), 188
Visual sensory channels, 23*fig*–24
Voice data delivery, 117–118
Voice (voice recognition), 44
VoIP (Voice over Internet Protocol), 49

W

W3C, 154
Wagner, Ellen, 164
WAN (wide area networks), 48
WAV (Waveform Audio), 154
Web 1.0 producer-generated content, 188;
    generations of the Web, 190*fig*
Web 2.0: 5-ables of, 189; generations of the
    Web, 190*fig*; social networking, 47, 87,
    102–103, 179, 180*t*, 188; user-generated
    content of, 188
Web 3.0: generations of the Web, 190*fig*;
    system-generated content, 189
Web browsing, 47
Wehlage, G., 79
*A Whole New Mind: Why Right-Brainers
    Will Rule the Future* (Pink), 17
Wi-fi connections, 48–49
WIIFM (What's in It for Me), 22, 144
Windows Mobile, 8
Windows operating system, 154, 156
Windows Phone (was Windows Mobile),
    156

Wireless networks: BREW (Binary
    Runtime Environment for Wireless), 159;
    mobile opportunities for, 108*t*, 179;
    Wi-fi connections, 48–49
Wolfram Alpha search engine, 189
Workforce mobility estimates, 8
WriteTechnology, 184

X

XHTML, 154
XML, 154

Y

Yahoo format, 47
YBCA (game), 91
Yerba Buena Center for the Arts (YBCA),
    91–93

Z

Zen of Palm: guiding mobile design,
    125–126; synergy between minimalism
    and, 137

Pfeiffer Publications Guide

This guide is designed to familiarize you with the various types of Pfeiffer publications. The formats section describes the various types of products that we publish; the methodologies section describes the many different ways that content might be provided within a product. We also provide a list of the topic areas in which we publish.

FORMATS

In addition to its extensive book-publishing program, Pfeiffer offers content in an array of formats, from fieldbooks for the practitioner to complete, ready-to-use training packages that support group learning.

FIELDBOOK Designed to provide information and guidance to practitioners in the midst of action. Most fieldbooks are companions to another, sometimes earlier, work, from which its ideas are derived; the fieldbook makes practical what was theoretical in the original text. Fieldbooks can certainly be read from cover to cover. More likely, though, you'll find yourself bouncing around following a particular theme, or dipping in as the mood, and the situation, dictate.

HANDBOOK A contributed volume of work on a single topic, comprising an eclectic mix of ideas, case studies, and best practices sourced by practitioners and experts in the field.

An editor or team of editors usually is appointed to seek out contributors and to evaluate content for relevance to the topic. Think of a handbook not as a ready-to-eat meal, but as a cookbook of ingredients that enables you to create the most fitting experience for the occasion.

RESOURCE Materials designed to support group learning. They come in many forms: a complete, ready-to-use exercise (such as a game); a comprehensive resource on one topic (such as conflict management) containing a variety of methods and approaches; or a collection of like-minded activities (such as icebreakers) on multiple subjects and situations.

TRAINING PACKAGE An entire, ready-to-use learning program that focuses on a particular topic or skill. All packages comprise a guide for the facilitator/trainer and a workbook for the participants. Some packages are supported with additional media—such as video—or learning aids, instruments, or other devices to help participants understand concepts or practice and develop skills.

- *Facilitator/trainer's guide* Contains an introduction to the program, advice on how to organize and facilitate the learning event, and step-by-step instructor notes. The guide also contains copies of presentation materials—handouts, presentations, and overhead designs, for example—used in the program.

- *Participant's workbook* Contains exercises and reading materials that support the learning goal and serves as a valuable reference and support guide for participants in the weeks and months that follow the learning event. Typically, each participant will require his or her own workbook.

ELECTRONIC CD-ROMs and web-based products transform static Pfeiffer content into dynamic, interactive experiences. Designed to take advantage of the searchability, automation, and ease-of-use that technology provides, our e-products bring convenience and immediate accessibility to your workspace.

METHODOLOGIES

CASE STUDY A presentation, in narrative form, of an actual event that has occurred inside an organization. Case studies are not prescriptive, nor are they used to prove a point; they are designed to develop critical analysis and decision-making skills. A case study has a specific time frame, specifies a sequence of events, is narrative in structure, and contains a plot structure—an issue (what should be/have been done?). Use case studies when the goal is to enable participants to apply previously learned theories to the circumstances in the case, decide what is pertinent, identify the real issues, decide what should have been done, and develop a plan of action.

ENERGIZER A short activity that develops readiness for the next session or learning event. Energizers are most commonly used after a break or lunch to stimulate or refocus the group. Many involve some form of physical activity, so they are a useful way to counter post-lunch lethargy. Other uses include transitioning from one topic to another, where "mental" distancing is important.

EXPERIENTIAL LEARNING ACTIVITY (ELA) A facilitator-led intervention that moves participants through the learning cycle from experience to application (also known as a Structured Experience). ELAs are carefully thought-out designs in which there is a definite learning purpose and intended outcome. Each step—everything that participants do during the activity—facilitates the accomplishment of the stated goal. Each ELA includes complete instructions for facilitating the intervention and a clear statement of goals, suggested group size and timing, materials required, an explanation of the process, and, where appropriate, possible variations to the activity. (For more detail on Experiential Learning Activities, see the Introduction to the *Reference Guide to Handbooks and Annuals*, 1999 edition, Pfeiffer, San Francisco.)

GAME A group activity that has the purpose of fostering team spirit and togetherness in addition to the achievement of a pre-stated goal. Usually contrived—undertaking a desert expedition, for example—this type of learning method offers an engaging means for participants to demonstrate and practice business and interpersonal skills. Games are effective for team building and personal development mainly because the goal is subordinate to the process—the means through which participants reach decisions, collaborate, communicate, and generate trust and understanding. Games often engage teams in "friendly" competition.

ICEBREAKER A (usually) short activity designed to help participants overcome initial anxiety in a training session and/or to acquaint the participants with one another. An icebreaker can be a fun activity or can be tied to specific topics or training goals. While a useful tool in itself, the icebreaker comes into its own in situations where tension or resistance exists within a group.

INSTRUMENT A device used to assess, appraise, evaluate, describe, classify, and summarize various aspects of human behavior. The term used to describe an instrument depends primarily on its format and purpose. These terms include survey, questionnaire, inventory, diagnostic, survey, and poll. Some uses of instruments include providing instrumental feedback to group members, studying here-and-now processes or functioning within a group, manipulating group composition, and evaluating outcomes of training and other interventions.

Instruments are popular in the training and HR field because, in general, more growth can occur if an individual is provided with a method for focusing specifically on his or her own behavior. Instruments also are used to obtain information that will serve as a basis for change and to assist in workforce planning efforts.

Paper-and-pencil tests still dominate the instrument landscape with a typical package comprising a facilitator's guide, which offers advice on administering the instrument and interpreting the collected data, and an initial set of instruments. Additional instruments are available separately. Pfeiffer, though, is investing heavily in e-instruments. Electronic instrumentation provides effortless distribution and, for larger groups particularly, offers advantages over paper-and-pencil tests in the time it takes to analyze data and provide feedback.

LECTURETTE A short talk that provides an explanation of a principle, model, or process that is pertinent to the participants' current learning needs. A lecturette is intended to establish a common language bond between the trainer and the participants by providing a mutual frame of reference. Use a lecturette as an introduction to a group activity or event, as an interjection during an event, or as a handout.

MODEL A graphic depiction of a system or process and the relationship among its elements. Models provide a frame of reference and something more tangible, and more easily remembered, than a verbal explanation. They also give participants something to "go on," enabling them to track their own progress as they experience the dynamics, processes, and relationships being depicted in the model.

ROLE PLAY A technique in which people assume a role in a situation/ scenario: a customer service rep in an angry-customer exchange, for example. The way in which the role is approached is then discussed and feedback is offered. The role play is often repeated using a different approach and/or incorporating changes made based on feedback received. In other words, role playing is a spontaneous interaction involving realistic behavior under artificial (and safe) conditions.

SIMULATION A methodology for understanding the interrelationships among components of a system or process. Simulations differ from games in that they test or use a model that depicts or mirrors some aspect of reality in form, if not necessarily in content. Learning occurs by studying the effects of change on one or more factors of the model. Simulations are commonly used to test hypotheses about what happens in a system—often referred to as "what if?" analysis—or to examine best-case/worst-case scenarios.

THEORY A presentation of an idea from a conjectural perspective. Theories are useful because they encourage us to examine behavior and phenomena through a different lens.

TOPICS

The twin goals of providing effective and practical solutions for workforce training and organization development and meeting the educational needs of training and human resource professionals shape Pfeiffer's publishing program. Core topics include the following:

> Leadership & Management
>
> Communication & Presentation
>
> Coaching & Mentoring
>
> Training & Development
>
> E-Learning
>
> Teams & Collaboration
>
> OD & Strategic Planning
>
> Human Resources
>
> Consulting

What will you find on pfeiffer.com?

- The best in workplace performance solutions for training and HR professionals

- Downloadable training tools, exercises, and content

- Web-exclusive offers

- Training tips, articles, and news

- Seamless on-line ordering

- Author guidelines, information on becoming a Pfeiffer Partner, and much more

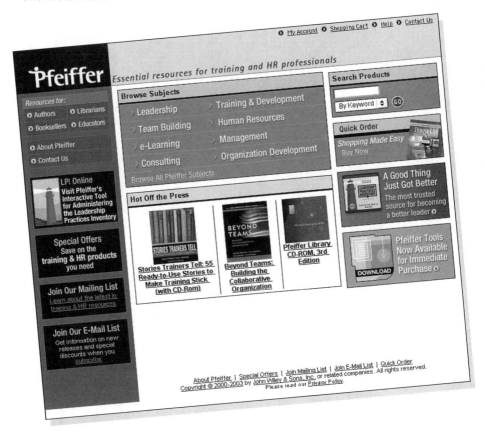

Discover more at www.pfeiffer.com